The
Vision
of the Void

THEOLOGICAL REFLECTIONS ON THE WORKS OF
ELIE WIESEL

BY

Michael Berenbaum

WESLEYAN UNIVERSITY PRESS
Middletown *Connecticut*

Copyright © 1979 by Michael Berenbaum

Library of Congress Cataloging in Publication Data

Berenbaum, Michael, 1945–
   The vision of the void.

      Bibliography: p.
      Includes index.
      1. Wiesel, Elie, 1928– —Religion and
ethics. 2. Holocaust (Jewish theology)
I. Title.
PQ2683.I32Z58   813'.5'4   78-27321
ISBN 0-8195-5030-2

Manufactured in the United States of America
First edition

For Linda's talents and Ilana's tears.

To Linda, who understands,
and to Ilana and Lev, who may come to understand.

Contents

Preface ix

Introduction 3

Chapter One: The Experience of the Void 9

Two: The Way Back 31

Three: *The Gates of the Forest*: The Partial Reconciliation with the Traditions of Israel 52

Four: The Memory of Mystery and the Mystery of Memory 69

Five: A Change of Perspective 91

Six: The Additional Covenant — Wiesel's Doctrine of Israel 125

Seven: Elie Wiesel and Contemporary Jewish Theology 152

Eight: Wiesel's Theory of the Holocaust 181

Bibliography 203

Index 213

Preface

THOUGH EVERY AUTHOR must assume final responsibility for his work, no work is ever solely the product of its author. I am deeply indebted to a number of people for their insights and inspiration and for their endeavors to critically assess the issues raised by this work. I owe a special debt of gratitude to Richard Rubenstein, the chairman of my doctoral committee and now a distinguished Professor of Religion at Florida State University, for being both a friend and a teacher and for having the wisdom to understand the difference. He taught me that a theological work must be uncompromisingly honest. It was in that spirit that we recognized quite early in our relationship that we might hold divergent views on a number of critical issues. The differences of views were always mutually respected. I have not only been privileged to study under a fine teacher, but in Talmudic fashion I have learned much from my gifted students at Wesleyan. To Jacob Calm, Jay Geller, Stephen Riegelhaupt, James Stahl, and Keith Stern I owe a great thanks, for it was in seminars with them that many of the ideas later incorporated into this work were first advanced. In teaching courses in Literature and Theology and in Modern

Jewish Thought over the past several years, further ideas were advanced and refined; many more were rejected. Consequently, I have been saved from many a peril. Debra Leah Salowitz-Storey has been of considerable help to me in typing an early draft of the book, and both she and her husband Neil painstakingly proofread the text. My secretary and friend Betty Lenth has seen this work more times than either she or I wish to recall, and I am grateful to her and to Louise Astin for their help with the manuscript.

I wish to thank Professor John Roth of Claremont Men's College for his theological engagement and for the care with which he read this work. I remember fondly the hours we spent in conversation on Wiesel's work. To my colleague David Swift I remain grateful for his encouragement, his concern, and his critical appreciation.

I must also express a most obvious but profound appreciation to Elie Wiesel. It is through my involvement with his work that I have been able to encounter not only his work but the author as well and to be enriched by both.

Words are insufficient to express my gratitude to my wife Linda for her help in this work. I am pleased that this work has brought us closer together and enabled us to explore painful but deeply important arenas of our own humanity. She has been of great help in working through the theological issues raised by this work. She has been an invaluable and constant critic of my efforts. For this and more I am more than grateful.

The inception of this work coincided with the birth of our daughter Ilana and its acceptance for publication with the birth of our son Lev. I am most pleased that the actual writing of the original draft of this work was completed in the Old City of Jerusalem within sight of the Western Wall. It is somehow appropriate that the work was completed in Jerusalem, the site of past Jewish glory, the focus

of Jewish hope, the locus of Israel's vitality, and the persistent reminder of continuing Jewish vulnerability.

Michael Berenbaum

Middletown, Connecticut
Yom Haatzmaut 5738

The Vision of the Void

Introduction

THE PAST four decades have been a time of unprecedented and ominous upheaval in Jewish life. Within this short span of time one-third of the Jewish people were killed, a Jewish state was founded, Jerusalem once again came under Jewish control, Soviet Jews experienced a resurgence of Jewish identity and self-consciousness, American Jewry proceeded further along the road to assimilation, and continued threats to the state of Israel once again proved its vulnerability and its dependence upon the good will of other nations. The religious consciousness of the Jewish people could not have remained unchanged throughout these tumultuous events. This work analyzes the changes in religious consciousness experienced by one deeply sensitive participant in these events.

Elie Wiesel was born in Sighet, a small Hungarian shtetl, on Simchat Torah (the fall festival of the rejoicing of the Torah) in 1928.[1] The third of four children and the only son, Wiesel was educated in Torah and sacred texts, spend-

1. The best source on Wiesel's life is *Harry James Cargas in Conversation with Elie Wiesel* (Paramus: The Paulist Press, 1976), pp. 62–80.

ing long hours at the *Heder* (the school room) and at a
Yeshiva. Wiesel has described his mother as a cultured
woman who combined deep piety with a secular education.
She had completed high school, which was somewhat rare
for a woman in the shtetl, and was fluent in German literature. She personified faith for Wiesel, and she hoped that
her son would become a Rabbi and a Ph.D. Wiesel's father
was a merchant, an emancipated yet observant Jew who
was an important figure in the Jewish community of Sighet
although a distant figure to his son until their incarceration
together in the camps. His father personified reason and
communal involvement.

At the age of fifteen Wiesel was taken off with his father
to Auschwitz and then to Buchenwald, where he remained
until his liberation from the camps on April 11, 1945. Wiesel
lost both his parents and his younger sister in the camps. He
and his older sisters survived the Nazi regime.

Following the war, Wiesel made his way to France
where he pursued his secondary education and later continued his studies at the Sorbonne in literature, psychology,
and philosophy. He began but never completed a long dissertation on comparative asceticism. While in Paris, Wiesel
worked as a correspondent for the Israeli afternoon newspaper, *Yediot Aharonot*. He moved to New York City in
1956 where he served as the United Nations correspondent
for *Yediot Aharonot*. He became an American citizen in
1963. As a correspondent, Wiesel twice traveled to the
Soviet Union, first in 1965 and a second time in 1966. He
traveled to Israel many times and was there during the
Six-Day War in 1967. In the mid-sixties he left journalism to
pursue his literary career full time. In 1972 he was ap-
pointed the Distinguished Professor of Jewish Studies at the
City College of New York, a position which he left in 1976
to assume the Andrew Mellon University Professorship at

Boston University. He married the former Marion Erster Rose, now his translator, in 1969, and their son Shlomo Elisha was born in 1972.

For every author, the use of language is critical. For Wiesel, an author to whom the nuances of language are of great significance, his experience with language has been quite unusual. Wiesel writes his literary work in French although his native tongue is Yiddish and the language of his native land was Hungarian. Throughout his career in journalism he wrote primarily in modern Hebrew, a language which he had learned in his childhood (outside of Israel) upon the insistence of his father. Although Wiesel has lived in the United States for twenty years, he learned his English in India while undertaking research for his unfinished dissertation. Nonetheless, Wiesel continues to write in French.

The bare outlines of Wiesel's life indicate that he has personally experienced all the major contemporary events that have shaped the Jewish consciousness. He sees himself and is seen by others as a witness and participant in each of these major events.

Wiesel's stature in the Jewish community is rather unique. Steven Schwarzschild, a former editor of *Judaism,* has called Wiesel "the *de facto* high priest of our generation."[2] According to Schwarzschild, Wiesel is the one man who speaks most tellingly of our time, of our hopes and fears, our tragedy and our protest. Wiesel has been termed a contemporary Rebbe,[3] the charismatic leader of our age. He has been called "the authentic Jew,"[4] the man who best

2. Steven Schwarzschild, "Toward Jewish Unity," *Judaism,* Vol. 15, No. 2 (Spring, 1966), p. 157.

3. Byron L. Sherwin, "Elie Wiesel and Jewish Theology," *Judaism,* Vol. 18, No. 1 (Winter, 1969), p. 52.

4. Edward Fiske, "Elie Wiesel, Activist with a Mission," *The New York Times,* January 31, 1973, p. 35.

embodies contemporary Jewish existence. He has also been called the witness of the Holocaust, the prophet and sage of Auschwitz. Emil Fackenheim, the distinguished Canadian Jewish theologian, has said of Wiesel: "His writings are forcing Jewish theological thought in our time into a new dimension."[5] The stature of Wiesel as a religious thinker is undoubtedly great, although the religious content of his works has not yet been treated systematically. In this work it is my intention to pursue a systematic treatment of Wiesel's religious thought.

Throughout my discussion of Wiesel's works the theological aspects and importance of his writing will be given careful attention. Embedded in the literary aspects of his work, in his imagery, symbols, language, and choice of forms, theological considerations are prominent. Wiesel's theology concentrates on the three pillars of Jewish thought: God, Israel, and Torah. (The concept of Torah is interpreted in the broadest sense to include tradition and the relationship to the past.)

Wiesel's theological vision is of the void. Where previous Jewish theologians found some security in God and His revelation, in man and his creaturely status, and in Israel and its divine mission, Wiesel now finds an abyss of chaos, madness, and radical insecurity. Wiesel's fundamental experience is one of absence in a world that was once pregnant with Presence. Where Wiesel formerly experienced God, he has come to encounter the void. This interpretation of Wiesel's writings will differ significantly from other interpretations. I shall consistently examine the points at which my interpretation differs from other interpretations and the reasons for my alternate analysis.

5. Emil Fackenheim, *God's Presence in History* (New York: New York University Press, 1969), p. v.

What many find compelling in Wiesel is the radical honesty of his writings and the struggle to find some sort of accommodation between the world of the tradition and the heterodoxy and heresy of contemporary experience. This honesty is especially evident in Wiesel's radicalness and his careful delimitation of the grounds for hope. Wiesel undercuts almost all positive images of God to such an extent that they are of limited use in defending Jewish theodicy. Essentially, Wiesel's writings force us to confront the void and to live in the limited and fragile domain of humanly created meaning.

This work will deal with all of Wiesel's published writings, now numbering seven novels, one memoir, three books of essays and short stories, two representations of Hasidic tales and one of Rabbinic legends, one cantata, and one play. I shall concentrate on the works that were most important in establishing Wiesel's theological position and his stature within the American Jewish community. I shall compare the essence of Wiesel's theological vision with the thought of other contemporary Jewish theologians, namely Emil Fackenheim, Richard Rubenstein, and Eliezer Berkovits, and shall consider his social and historical understanding of the Holocaust in comparison to the treatments of Bruno Bettelheim, Lucy Dawidowicz, Hannah Arendt, and Raul Hilberg. In these comparisons the uniqueness of Wiesel's vision and its radical implications will become apparent.

Different levels of Wiesel's work will be elucidated through their relationship to Jewish tradition and through a psycho-social interpretation. Although I draw from sociological and psychoanalytic categories, I endeavor to treat Wiesel's writings textually without distorting his work by the imposition of foreign categories. In my treatment of Wiesel I adhere to an inductive method. I shall emphasize

Wiesel's insights while letting his writings tell their own tale.[6]

6. The failure to treat Wiesel's statements within their literary context runs the risk of a serious distortion of both the form that he has chosen for the material and its content. One may not say, "Wiesel says . . ." without specifying the context, the medium (novel, conversation, lecture, short story, rabbinic legend). In his fictional works the relationship between the characters and the author must always be considered.

Chapter One

The Experience of the Void

ALL OF Wiesel's writings are concerned with the ramifications of the Holocaust for man, God, and Israel. Peter Berger has argued that death is the marginal experience *par excellence* which threatens to reveal the innate precariousness of all socially constructed universes.[1] If death is the marginal experience *par excellence,* then the death of six million Jews in the Holocaust is the marginal experience *extraordinaire* which has undermined the socially constructed universe of normative Judaism. Wiesel's writings are an attempt to come to terms with that marginal experience and to construct a new universe to replace the one that was shattered.

The progression in Wiesel's first three novels, *Night, Dawn,* and *Le Jour (The Accident),*[2] from night to dawn to day, is not merely a positive progression from a world of darkness to a world of light, but also a progression from a

1. Peter Berger, *The Sacred Canopy*(Garden City: Doubleday and Company, Inc., 1967), pp. 43–44.
2. The translation of *Le Jour* as *The Accident* seems to be a quirk of its English publication. Although the work appeared in both a Dutch and a Hebrew translation, both maintained the title as *Day.* To maintain a sense of the trilogy, I consistently refer to *The Accident* as *Le Jour.*

world in which God is present (at the beginning of *Night*), to a world in which God is killed so that man can live (in *Dawn*), and finally to a world in which God is absent (in *Le Jour*). In *Le Jour* God's presence is no longer felt, and the individual lives without meaning and without God. It is ironic that Wiesel's titles become brighter as the presence of God becomes dimmer, but this irony reflects Wiesel's reliance upon man in a world devoid of God. Nonetheless, the transition from a God-filled world to a Godless world is not easy for Wiesel. He continually emphasizes not only the initial suffering that brought him to his view of a Godless world, but also the internal pain that accompanies this new consciousness. He yearns to return to the God-filled world and to the shtetl in the Carpathian Mountains from which he was prematurely snatched and taken into the kingdom of night.

Theodicy in *Night*

There are few better illustrations of Hegel's famous statement that "history is the slaughter bench at which the happiness of peoples, the wisdom of states and the virtue of individuals have been sacrificed"[3] than Wiesel's 1958 memoir *Night*.[4] In *Night* Wiesel vividly describes the transition from belief to disillusionment. At the beginning of

3. G. W. F. Hegel, *Reason in History: A General Introduction to the Philosophy of History,* trans. with an introduction by Robert S. Hartman (New York: The Liberal Arts Press, 1953), p. 27.
4. Wiesel has stressed that *Night* is a memoir, and he vouches for the veracity of his descriptions. Originally published in Yiddish as *Un Di Velt Hot Geshvign* (And the World has Remained Silent) (Buenos Aires: Y el Mundo Callaba, Central Farbond Fun Poylishe Yidn in Argentina, 1956), this work was later condensed into the French Edition de Minuit version as *La Nuit*. The English edition of *Night* was first published in New York in 1960 by Hill and Wang and has since become a classic of Holocaust literature.

Night Wiesel's world is dominated by his involvement with God. The author describes himself as a young boy who is fascinated by the mystery of God's transcendence and yearns to bring about the awaited redemption. The young boy studies the Talmud by day and the mysteries of the Kabbalah by night. He rises at midnight to keep the *Shekinah*[5] company, for she is in exile, and he weeps bitterly over the destruction of the Temple and the exile of both Israel and God. The boy's life and faith were one. When asked why he prays, the boy was puzzled by the question. "Why did I pray? A strange question. Why did I live? Why did I breathe?"[6] He was aware of the contradictions and the questions of historical existence, but like Rabbi Nachman of Bratzlav, he withstood the questions with a staunch faith that looked toward the dimension of eternity, the level at which question and answer were one.[7]

Wiesel begins to reveal an erosion of faith when he describes its deceptive power. He explains that in Sighet, the Transylvanian town of his youth, the signs of the imminent slaughter were apparent, but that only the discerning eyes of a few — a madman, a visionary, and a prophet, or those who had seen the end and returned to tell the tale —

5. In the Jewish mystical tradition the *Shekinah* is the divine presence.

6. Elie Wiesel, *Night* (New York: Avon Books, 1960), p. 13.

7. For the best treatment of the role of the question in the thought of Rabbi Nachman of Bratzlav, see J. G. Weiss, "The Question in the Teaching of Rabbi Nachman of Bratzlav," *Zion,* Vol. 16 (1951). Much can be said of Wiesel's indebtedness to Rabbi Nachman in both the method and the content of his trilogy. Both are tortured souls yearning for renewed innocence and both approach the world with a great deal of skepticism. Both share a fascination with the Messiah and the ability of man to force God's hand. However, Rabbi Nachman's questions point toward their resolution in the leap of faith, while Wiesel's questions remain forever questions. For an excellent understanding of Rabbi Nachman see Arthur E. Green, *Rabbi Nachman of Bratzlav: A Critical Biography* (University: The University of Alabama Press, forthcoming).

could really face the truth. For the rest of the community, and for the author himself, an illusion of safety prevailed and life continued normally. The illusion of a merciful universe sustained some people, faith in humanity nourished the hopes of others, while for Wiesel the lure of eternity clouded his sense of reality. Tragically, it was faith and not wickedness that misled the people of Sighet.

As the story of *Night* unfolds, Wiesel describes how his faith was slowly and painfully consumed by the flames that sent the souls of the young and the innocent skyward. Wiesel's faith and the faith of many of the characters he describes had been fortified against the encroachment of anomic forces by the teachings of Jewish tradition. In other words, Wiesel was not psychically unarmed to confront the problem of evil that the concentration camp experience raised. He knew both the history of the problem within Jewish tradition and the many possible defenses against the incursion of *anomie*. However, none of these defenses ultimately worked for Wiesel on an existential level, and it is on the existential level that the religious problem of evil must be faced. (The theoretical problem can easily be resolved by either challenging God's goodness, diminishing His power, or denying His existence.) Through the incidents and reflections presented in *Night,* Wiesel undermines the traditional strategies for explaining and handling the presence of evil.

One traditional strategy of the Rabbis for preserving the belief in God's justice is expressed in the prayer book for the Holidays. This strategy is a moral one which seeks to understand the historical situation of Israel in light of its wrongdoings and its evil ways. According to this strategy, Israel has sinned and consequently must be punished: "Because of our sins we were exiled from our land."[8] How-

8. The phrase "Because of our sins we were exiled from the land" is the standard introduction to the recitation of the sacrificial requirements

ever, Wiesel is unable to accept this strategy. He never even entertains the possibility that the iniquities of the people led to their annihilation. In fact, Wiesel angrily rejects this strategy. Speaking of his teachers, he said:

I had another teacher who taught me to sing . . . . He taught me a song *U'mipnai Chata'enu,* it is because of our sins that we had been exiled. I sang it then. I sing it now, and now I resent it. No, it is not because of our sins. There were no sins, not that many. I refuse to believe that there could have been so many sins to provoke such a punishment. If there was such a punishment, it is because someone else had sinned, not we, not the people of Israel.[9]

---

in the additional service of all major Jewish festivals. It not only suggests the reason for Jewish exile, but also proposes a political strategy for returning to the land and ending exile. Obedience to God is the means by which exile can be ended.

9. Elie Wiesel, "My Teachers," a radio address on the NBC Radio Network, Sunday, April 8, 1973; as part of the Eternal Light Series of the Jewish Theological Seminary, New York: The Jewish Theological Seminary, 1973.

Others have not been as cautious about their assessment of blame to the Jewish people. There are three well-known cases where blame has been assigned to the Jewish people. See "The Dean and the Chosen People" in Richard L. Rubenstein's *After Auschwitz* (Indianapolis: Bobbs-Merrill, 1966), pp. 47–61, in which Rubenstein describes his meeting with Dean Gruber, an anti-Nazi Christian leader, who spoke of the Jews and the Holocaust in the Biblical perspective of sin and punishment. The Hasidic master known as "the Satmer Rebbe" is said to believe that the Holocaust is God's punishment of the Jewish people for the sin of Zionism (which for him represents the refusal to wait for God to bring the Messiah and restore the Jewish people to their land). Professor Zalman Schacter has written:

In response to Nazi hostilities, we judged all Germans to be inhuman, predatory beasts, and the Germans returned the compliment. They were stronger, and we, by definition, the vermin to be exterminated. In short, the Holocaust was partially caused by Jews who did not think it worthwhile, or even possible, to reprove the Germans. (*The Religious Situation, 1968,* D. R. Cutler, ed. [Boston: Beacon Press, 1968], p. 81.)

Wiesel never employs this type of strategy to preserve the theodicy of Israel.

By rejecting this explanation, Wiesel refuses to relieve God of His responsibility. Both Wiesel's love of Israel and his respect for the God that Israel revered precluded that possibility.

Another traditional strategy for explaining the existence of evil seeks to defer ultimate justice to the time of the Messiah or the world to come. One such strategy is put most succinctly by Raba, the Babylonian *amora* (sage) of the fourth generation, who said that Job's sin was his lack of belief in the resurrection of the dead.[10] Job's complaint could only arise in a situation where historical existence is considered the sole form of existence and where life itself is expected to be rewarding. The Jewish view that the Messiah will restore Israel serves as a powerful force for defending the plausibility structure of Judaism by deferring justice and reward to a future time. In the words of Gershom Scholem, the Jewish view of the Messiah is "a theory of catastrophe."[11] It would seem that this theory is most applicable in the presence of catastrophes. Wiesel realizes the healing potential of the belief in a messianic solution, but he seems to reject the ultimate reality of such a solution or its ability to 'explain' or 'dismiss' the present. Wiesel's style of writing itself emphasizes the reality of present experiences as opposed to explanation or abstract analysis. Wiesel primarily chooses to describe rather than to explain. He thereby lets his incidents tell their own tale. Experience speaks louder than explanations and cannot be silenced by answers. Furthermore, Wiesel's treatment of the theologi-

10. Baba Batra 16a. All quotations from the Babylonian Talmud are taken from *The Babylonian Talmud,* translated under the editorship of I. Epstein, 37 volumes (London and Bournemouth: Soncino Press, 1935–52). The quotations are indicated according to the tractate and the Hebrew page.

11. Gershom Scholem, *The Messianic Idea in Judaism* (New York: Schocken Books, 1971), p. 7.

cal explanations themselves reveals their lack of connection with the experiences they seek to explain.

This discontinuity is illustrated by Wiesel's description of a conversation among the inmates shortly after their arrival at Auschwitz.

In the evening, lying on our beds, we would try to sing some of the Hasidic melodies, and Akiba Drumer would break our hearts with his deep, solemn voice.

Some talked of God, of his mysterious ways, of the sins of the Jewish people, and of their future deliverance. But I had ceased to pray. How I sympathized with Job! I did not deny God's existence, but I doubted His absolute justice.

Akiba Drumer said: "God is testing us. He wants to find out whether we can dominate our base instincts and kill the Satan within us. We have no right to despair. And if he punishes us relentlessly, it's a sign that He loves us all the more."

Hersch Genud, well versed in the cabbala, spoke of the end of the world and the coming of the Messiah.

Only occasionally during these conversations did the thought occur to me: "Where is my mother at this moment? And Tzipora . . . ?[12]

Although this discussion may have distracted the young Wiesel from his terrible plight, it hardly spoke to his reality. The author's juxtaposition of the discussion of theology and his recollection of his infrequent thoughts of his family emphasizes the lack of connection between the two. The distinction between the historical present and the messianic future did help to sustain individual communities through their misery and thus helped to preserve not only the individual but the belief in Judaism as well. However, Wiesel cannot accept messianism as an alternative to facing the Holocaust nor can he accept a Messiah who refused to

12. *Night*, pp. 55–56.

appear at the time when he was so crucially needed.[13] After the experience of Auschwitz, Wiesel was forced to take history with the utmost seriousness. It became for him the principal level of existence.[14] The Rabbinic strategies, which deferred the explanation of evil until the messianic future or the world to come, did not work for Wiesel. Wiesel had once been prepared for eternity; his life was shattered by history.

The Zohar, the central Kabbalistic text in Jewish mysticism, presents a third strategy for defending the traditional theodicy in the face of evil. The Zohar relates the following parable:

It is the will of the Holy One that men should worship Him and walk in the way of truth that they may be rewarded with many benefits. How, then, can an evil servant come and counteract the will of his Master by tempting man to walk in an evil way, seducing him from the good way and causing him to disobey the will of his Lord? But, indeed, the "evil inclination" also does this through the will of its Lord. It is as if a king had an only son whom he dearly loved, and just for that cause he warned him not to be enticed by bad women, saying that anyone defiled might not enter his palace. The son promised his father to do his will in love. Outside the palace, however, there lived a beautiful harlot. After a while the King thought: "I will see how far my son is devoted to me." So he sent to the woman and commanded her, saying: "Entice my son, for I wish to test his obedience to my will." So she used every blandishment to lure him into her embraces.[15]

13. See my discussion of the Messiah.
14. It is precisely on this point that Wiesel's position differs from the views of Emil Fackenheim (in his early works) and Franz Rosenzweig. Fackenheim was searching for a religious faith immune from the vicissitudes of history, and Rosenzweig extolled the Jews as removed from history, gazing upon eternity.
15. Zohar II 163a. All quotations from the Zohar are taken from *The Zohar,* translated by Harry Sperling, Maurice Simon, and Paul P. Lever-

According to this parable, evil is God's test of Israel's love and obedience. Evil tempts people to renounce or abandon God's moral commandments. Thus, evil is viewed as a part of God's greater plan, and the nature of the evil itself is denied ultimate significance. Evil becomes a creation of God in service of a greater good. Wiesel rejects this explanation of the Holocaust for many of the same reasons he rejected the first two explanations. In addition to the negative characterization that would have to be ascribed to a God who would devise such a 'test' as the Holocaust, the text explanation, like the messianic explanation, does not really relate to the actual experience of suffering. Like the other theological explanations, the concept of the test leads the mind away from the reality that raised the question of evil rather than speaking to that reality. Thus, Wiesel's existential situation could not be explained by traditional theology, and he therefore lost his faith in the traditional solutions. These solutions were ultimately ineffective in lessening his suffering or in protecting him from the encroachment of anomie.

Wiesel describes in *Night* how he first expressed his rejection of traditional theology in terms of religious rebellion. He was shocked by the incongruity of a liturgy that praised God and a reality that indicted Him. Wiesel refused to repress this incongruity and therefore defiantly refused to praise God. Wiesel describes how the new arrivals at Auschwitz began to recite Kaddish when they came to recognize the true nature of their situation. The Kaddish, a prayer in praise of God that is recited by the mourner following the death of a close relative, symbolically serves

---

toff, 5 volumes (London: Soncino Press, 1933). All quotations are indicated by the Hebrew volume and pagination.

as a proclamation of God's justice in the face of death. Wiesel was revolted at this recitation. He writes:

> For the first time, I felt revolt rise up in me. Why should I bless His name? The Eternal, Lord of the Universe, the All-Powerful and Terrible, was silent. What had I to thank Him for?[16]

Yet moments later, in spite of himself, Wiesel began to pray. He could not dismiss God so he confronted and condemned Him. In one prayer, for example, he thanked God for the magnificence of the universe in which mud could hide the shine of even a new pair of shoes. Wiesel continued to express this feeling of revolt against God throughout the book.

As Wiesel's anger intensified, his rebellion became defiance. The author describes the New Year services in the camps, services in which God is proclaimed King and is praised for recalling His covenant with Israel and in which Israel is praised as the Chosen of God. Wiesel became angered at his fellow inmates for having surrendered to the drama of the liturgy and for still being troubled (as indeed he himself still was) by the question of God or, perhaps more accurately, by the burden of God. The juxtaposition of the New Year liturgy and the reality of Auschwitz proved an outrage to Wiesel. In rebellion, he refused to bless God's name and to praise a universe in which there were factories of death and in which Israel was the chosen victim. Wiesel describes the service and his rejection of it.

> "All creation bears witness to the Greatness of God!"
> Once, New Year's Day had dominated my life. I knew that my sins grieved the Eternal; I implored his forgiveness. Once, I had believed profoundly that upon one solitary deed of mine, one solitary prayer, depended the salvation of the world.

16. *Night*, p. 43.

This day I had ceased to plead. I was no longer capable of lamentation. On the contrary, I felt very strong. I was the accuser, God the accused. My eyes were open and I was alone — terribly alone in a world without God and without man. Without love or mercy. . . . I stood amid that praying congregation, observing it like a stranger.[17]

In this passage Wiesel reveals how he had moved beyond rebellion and defiance to alienation and radical loneliness. This sense of estrangement is not confined to Wiesel's immediate experience in the camps nor to his descriptions of that experience in *Night*.[18] He returns to the feeling of alienation time and again in his novels and short stories. The alienation that Wiesel describes involves not only a severance from eternity but an integral involvement in history. Thus, the drama of the New Year in the camps which he describes in *Night* was not played out in the domain of the divine but in the human arena.

Wiesel further undercuts the divine-human encounter of Yom Kippur, the encounter in which the individual stands naked before God and asks that his deeds be examined and that he be judged for life, by choosing to describe Yom Kippur as the day for a selection by the earthly masters, the S.S. The penitents who had besieged the Lord with prayer the evening before were forced to test their skills on far more attentive masters as they tried to pass an inspection by the S.S. doctor who had within *his* power the decision of life and death. Wiesel describes how the S.S. made Yom Kippur into a Day of Judgment where the fate of men was decided by their masters. The drama of the Day of Judg-

17. *Ibid.*, p. 79.
18. See Wiesel's description of his visit to a Manhattan synagogue frequented by Professor Abraham Joshua Heschel in his "Excerpts from a Diary," in *One Generation After* (New York: Random House, 1970), pp. 242–249.

ment came true in a manner never envisioned by the tradition.

Wiesel's rebellion in *Night* is not limited to diatribes alone. Wiesel describes the arrival of the Day of Atonement, the sacred day of judgment, when he was forced to express his rebellion and alienation in deed as well as in thought. He was forced to question whether he should eat on Yom Kippur, whether one should fast in the camps. He wrestled painfully with the place of tradition and obedience in the world of night. Wiesel resolved the question by eating. He describes the occasion:

> . . . there was no longer any reason why I should fast. I no longer accepted God's silence. As I swallowed my bowl of soup, I saw in the gesture an act of rebellion and protest against Him.
>
> And I nibbled my crust of bread.
> In the depths of my heart, I felt a great void.[19]

The void of personal separation from God, the void of meaninglessness in life, and the void of God's absence in history are all acutely expressed by the author. In a sense, the entire corpus of Wiesel's writings is an attempt to confront absence, to describe the beauty that preceded it, the pain of separation, the yearning for return, and the failure of all efforts to return.

The void that Wiesel experienced was precipitated by the gap between his religion and his reality, between the realm of eternity and the realm of history. Throughout *Night* he underscores his rejection of faith by contrasting the reality of pain with the language of liturgy and with the hopes generated by faith. Each of the characters Wiesel develops feels the acute anxiety of disappointment. None survive with their faith intact. Old Rabbis declare their heretical feelings. Akiba Drumer, a formerly pious man,

19. *Night,* p. 80.

abandons his belief in both God and life. Mercifully, others die before they can fully lose their faith. The author survives, having witnessed the "other side"[20] of man and God, feeling the abyss of a Godless world and the guilt of knowing that he has both betrayed others and been the victim himself of betrayal. He alone must look in the mirror and begin again, if only to tell his tale.

Theodicy in *Dawn*

Wiesel's second novel, *Dawn*, was first published in France in 1960. The novel is set in Palestine just prior to the foundation of the state of Israel. Elisha, the protagonist of the novel, is the chosen executioner of a British soldier, Captain Dawson, whose life is to be taken in retaliation for the execution of a young Jewish terrorist.

Elisha is a fomer concentration camp inmate who later became a student of philosophy in order to understand the perennial questions of eternity and to ascribe blame to man and God for the events that so marred his adolescence.[21] Elisha's course of studies in Paris was interrupted by a Sabra, a native-born Palestinian Jew, who wished to solicit him for a terrorist organization and train him in the art of force. Elisha's solicitor took him to Palestine where he met his new master who instructed him in the art of combat, an art that did not allow him to discern cosmic patterns but that provided him with a new sense of power and control over his fate. During his period of training, Elisha was

20. The "other side" is the English rendition of the technical term in the Jewish mystical tradition *sitra achara*. It is another term for evil in that it negates the Godhead through separation.

21. The parallels between the author and his protagonist are marked, but *Dawn* is not a memoir but rather a novel. Methodologically, one should be careful to distinguish between the author and his protagonist and not to assume identity.

forced to undergo a radical change in both his character and aspirations. He finally qualified as a terrorist.

The central theme explored by Wiesel in *Dawn* is the relationship between God's dominion and man's obedience. In *Night* God does not intervene to save His people and enforce His laws. In *Dawn* Wiesel describes how man obliterated God's dominion when he tried to enforce justice himself and how he destroyed his trust in God in order to save himself.

The story Wiesel tells in *Dawn* details how the establishment of the state of Israel and the new reliance of the Jewish people on their own power involves a rejection of the God of Israel who was expected to reveal himself through history. Although Elisha does not fully understand his confrontation with God, it is primarily this conquest of God through complete self-reliance that is taught him by his terrorist master. During his instruction Elisha recalls an earlier master who had taught him Kabbalah before the war. Elisha recounts some of his teachings and presents his reaction to it.

> I remembered how the grizzled master had explained the sixth commandment to me. Why has a man no right to commit murder? Because in so doing he takes upon himself the function of God. And this must not be done too easily. Well, I said to myself, *if in order to change the course of our history we have to become God, we shall become Him. How easy that is we shall see. No, it was not easy.*[22] (italics mine)

People must act in order to affect history. People must create in a world functionally devoid of God, a world that does not turn to God for salvation. Wiesel restates this point even more explicitly in a later work with reference to the state of Israel during a situation of war. "Whoever kills,

22. Elie Wiesel, *Dawn* (New York: Hill and Wang, 1961), p. 30.

becomes God. Whoever kills, kills God. Each murder is a suicide, with the Eternal eternally the victim."[23] In order to live and shape history, in order to be independent and self-reliant, humanity must kill its sense of reliance upon God and affect its own salvation.[24]

The climax of *Dawn* comes near the end of the novel when Elisha must finally confirm the course of his training and the degree of his transformation by executing a British hostage. Elisha is convinced that this execution is necessary to insure the foundation of an independent Jewish state in Palestine. In the final scene of the novel, after Elisha has executed his victim, he comes to the realization that he himself was the victim. Elisha considers the situation: "That's it, I said to myself. It's done. I've killed. I've killed Elisha."[25]

The interpretation of this passage beyond the literal level hinges on the meaning of the name Elisha. It is obvious that in killing another person Elisha has also killed a part of himself, but I am convinced that Wiesel implies far more by this passage than is immediately apparent. To elucidate the meaning of Elisha's critical statement, it is important to consider the significance of names themselves within the Jewish tradition for this tradition is so much a part of Wiesel's idiom. The importance of names for Wiesel can be verified by reference to his use of them in his other works. In connection with this work, the specific meaning of the name Elisha, in addition to the implied reference to the two famous Elishas in Jewish tradition, exposes deeper levels of meaning in Elisha's climactic statement.

23. Elie Wiesel, *A Beggar in Jerusalem* (New York: Random House, 1970), p. 208.
24. One of the problems with some theologies of waiting for God is that they lead to a politics of self-restraint and passivity. Israel represents a politics of action and assertion.
25. *Dawn*, p. 89.

A glance at some of Wiesel's other novels reveals that Wiesel chooses his names very carefully for their historical overtones and for their exact meaning in Hebrew. In *The Town Beyond the Wall,* for example, the central character's name is Michael, and the name Michael, *Mi ca el*, in Hebrew literally means "who is like God." Throughout the novel, Michael in fact struggles to achieve the strength and omnipotence of God. In addition, when considered in the interrogative "who is like God?" Michael's name expresses the central question that remains unresolved throughout the novel. Similarly, in *A Beggar in Jerusalem* the narrator's name, David, is particularly significant. The name David reinforces many of the historical and messianic overtones present throughout the novel for the name connotes not merely the legendary king of Israel who captured Jerusalem and made it his capital, but also the Messiah who, according to tradition, will be a descendant of David. Wiesel's emphasis on the significance of names themselves[26] is an extension of the importance of names within Jewish tradition for, according to Jewish lore, names are thought to reveal the essence of one's being.

Within Jewish literature the specific name Elisha is held by two important figures, the prophet Elisha who was the successor of Elijah, and Elisha ben Abuyah, the heretic who was the teacher of Rabbi Meir and an important man in his own right. Elisha the prophet was not only the principal

26. In *The Gates of the Forest* the narrator comments:

Names played an important part in creation . . . . It was by naming things that God made them . . . . You admit, then, that a name has a fate of its own, independent of the life and fate of its bearer. Sometimes a name ages, falls ill, and dies much before the man who bears it. (Elie Wiesel, *The Gates of the Forest* [New York: Holt, Rinehart & Winston, 1966], pp. 9–10.)

See also Wiesel's discussion of names in *Messengers of God* (New York: Random House, 1976).

successor of Elijah but his faithful companion as well. According to Rabbinic lore, Elisha was both a disciple and a colleague who surpassed his master as a miracle worker by performing sixteen miracles (twice the number performed by Elijah). These miracles ranged from crossing the river and healing the leper to reviving the dead.[27] Elisha the heretic was a contemporary of Rabbi Akivah and one of the four rabbis to enter the sacred realm of mystery. Of the four rabbis, only Akivah emerged unscathed. Ben Zoma went mad, Ben Azzai died, and Elisha lost his faith.[28] According to some Rabbinic traditions, Elisha is depicted as a dualist. According to others, his apostasy was a total denial of the theodicy of Israel. Elisha once declared: the world is "let din v'let dayan,"[29] without justice and without a judge. Ironically, the name Elisha itself has the literal Hebrew meaning "God will save."

Theodicy in *Le Jour*

The struggle between life and death continues to dominate Wiesel's third novel of the trilogy, *Le Jour*. However, in this novel alone God is not implicated either in life or in death. In *Night* God was implicated in the anguish of the living as He was in the extermination of the dead. In *Dawn* God was implicated in the death of Captain Dawson. The execution was in fact the execution of God. In *Le Jour*, however, the struggle is no longer between man and God or even between man and man. The struggle is within Eliezer, now a newspaper correspondent for an Israeli paper. The battle rages between Eliezer's desire to live and create and his yearning for death and peace.

27. See Louis Ginzberg, *The Legends of the Jews*, Vol. IV (Philadelphia: Jewish Publications Society, 1913), pp. 237–246.
28. *Haggigah* 14b.
29. *Ibid.*

The battle between life and death is constant in *Le Jour*. The accident that brought Eliezer to the brink of death was in fact not an accident but rather the occasion chosen subconsciously by the correspondent to dramatize the battle waging within him. After the accident, a lover, a friend, the sky, and the light help retain the correspondent's thin hold on life, while his mother and grandmother, the sea, and the rivers tempt him to yield to death. Fever and physical pain combine with his emotional suffering and with his sense of fragmentation to battle for death while a pragmatic American doctor struggles to preserve his life. The doctor tells the correspondent:

> "Every man is like the river . . . Rivers flow toward the sea, which is never full. Men are swallowed up by death which is never satiated."[30]

Yet, in spite of himself, Eliezer repeats Dylan Thomas' famous line, ". . . rage, rage, against the dying of the light."[31]

Both the historical references and the literal meaning of the name Elisha are relevant to the character Elisha in *Dawn*. The image of a pupil who comes to equal if not surpass his master (particularly if his master is The Master) and who has learned to work his own miracles, as well as the image of a heretic who has lost his faith and expresses that loss either in dualism or denial are both images that relate to Wiesel's Elisha. (In addition, the miracles performed by the prophet Elisha are symbolically relevant to the story in *Dawn*. The crossing of the river recalls both the Exodus and the entrance into the promised land and can thus be applied to the foundation of the state of Israel as the

30. Elie Wiesel, *The Accident* (New York: Hill and Wang, 1962), p. 57.
31. *Ibid.*, p. 16.

return to the promised land. The healing of the leper can represent the leprous isolation of the Jewish people throughout the Holocaust by the other nations of the world and the end to the isolation that the foundation of the state of Israel seemed to provide. Most powerfully, the revival of the dead can represent the revival of the Jewish people after the catastrophic destruction of the Holocaust.) Furthermore, the literal Hebrew meaning of the name Elisha, which refers to a saving God, is most relevant to Wiesel's Elisha. If we apply these historical and literal references to Elisha's crucial statement "I've killed Elisha," additional levels of meaning appear in the statement. When Elisha and his Jewish compatriots consent to war and killing in order to form a state, we must ask ourselves whom they really have killed. Which Elisha has been killed? Does the foundation of the state of Israel by violence entail the death of Elisha the prophet who revives the dead? Does the assumption of power by the Jewish people and their own enforcement of justice by violence entail the end of Elisha the heretic who proclaimed there was no justice? Does the foundation of the state of Israel signify an act of deicide, the murder of Elisha, the saving God? It is my belief that the execution that Elisha commits primarily signifies an act of deicide. The price for the historical survival of the Jewish people involves the functional death (if not the deliberate murder) of a saving God.

As Elisha learns, deicide is never an easy act to commit. Although he recognizes the necessity of doing without God in order to affect history, this recognition is not without its inner turmoil. Elisha knows that there can be no return to the sacred cosmos of the past, yet in the very depths of his being he never ceases to yearn for a return to such a cosmos.

What is God's role in such a universe? The narrator of

Le Jour relates the difference between his first and second experience in surgery. During his first experience, when the narrator was still a child, he dreamed of approaching the heavenly throne and of asking the questions that have always been sacred mysteries to Israel. "When will the exile end?" "When will the anointed one, the Messiah, come?" The narrator distinctly remembers the fact that God did respond, although when he awoke he could not recall the content of the response. There were answers to his questions, and even if he did not remember the answers later, he knew that there was a realm where question and answer were one. By the time the narrator undergoes his second experience in surgery, he has become an adult. After this surgery the narrator relates to the doctor, "I didn't see God in my dream. He was no longer there."[32] God's absence during the second experience was as pronounced as His presence had formerly been.

If there is a God in *Le Jour,* He is not the God of Israel, a just and saving God, but rather a compassionless sadist. The correspondent explains:

Man prefers to blame himself for all possible sins and crimes rather than come to the conclusion that God is capable of the most flagrant injustice. I still blush every time I think of the way God makes fun of human beings, his favorite toys.[33]

Wiesel continues to elaborate his negative image of God by citing a concept from Lurrianic Kabbalism and then twisting it into a demonic form. In Lurrianic Kabbalism, God was considered dependent upon humanity in order to become one again. Human salvation and God's liberation were integrally related. In a bitter passage the correspondent reaffirms God's dependence upon man and God's radical loneliness. However, God is now depicted as de-

32. *Ibid.,* p. 71–72.
33. *Ibid.,* p. 41.

pendent upon humanity solely for entertainment and diversion:

Yes, God needs man. Condemned to eternal solitude, he made man only to use him as a toy, to amuse himself. That's what philosophers and poets have refused to admit: in the beginning there was neither the Word, nor Love, but laughter, the roaring, eternal laughter whose echoes are more deceitful than the mirages of the desert.[34]

The correspondent's deliberate denunciation of God establishes the distance between him and the theodicy of traditional Judaism, and the ontological structure that he chooses in place of the tradition does not insulate him against death. The victory of life at the end of the novel is in no way assured. Wiesel wishes to illustrate that the outcome of any individual battle is uncertain, that it is in fact 'accidental.' Even if life wins the immediate battle, death cannot be overcome. Death ultimately triumphs. Though the correspondent does rage against death and though he does outwit death a second time, the external forces of death and his own desire for death do remain. The ashes of the past will inevitably return to haunt him as they have haunted him before. All being is being unto death. In *Le Jour* Wiesel exposes a world in which God is at best absent in the struggle between life and death. At worst, God may even be an ally of the forces of death.

Conclusions

The questions that preoccupied Wiesel in *Night* concerning the suffering of the innocent and the absence of redemption

34. *Ibid.*, p. 42. Compare this passage with Wiesel's statement in the Judaism symposium "On Jewish Values in the Post-Holocaust Future" in which Wiesel claimed, "In the beginning was Auschwitz," or with I. B. Singer's statement in *Enemies: A Love Story*, "In the beginning was lust."

are harshly answered in *Le Jour*. Wiesel explains that there is no reason why the innocent suffer and that the hour of redemption is death. This is the sad truth that humanity avoids and tries to repress at all costs.

Men cast aside the one who has known pure suffering, if they cannot make a god out of him; the one who tells them: I suffered not because I was God, nor because I was a saint trying to imitate Him, but only because I am a man, a man like you, with your weaknesses, your cowardice, your sins, your rebellions, and your ridiculous ambitions; such a man frightens men, because he makes them feel ashamed. They pull away from him as if he were guilty. As if he were usurping God's place to illuminate the great vacuum that we find at the end of all adventures.[35]

In the beginning as night descended there was hope and faith. In the end when the day arrived there is a vacuum, death. The trilogy of *Night, Dawn,* and *Le Jour* marks the transition from a God-infused world to a Godless world, the transition from a world in which redemption can be expected to one in which all that is left is to rage against the dying of the light. Surely no critic who has carefully read these three volumes can see in them a vision of hope and a restoration of the sacred cosmos of normative Judaism. At this stage in his writing, Wiesel affirms human finitude in a world unconducive to the ultimate realization of human desires.

35. *Ibid.*, pp. 105–106.

Chapter Two

The Way Back

IT IS WITH the burning of the past that Wiesel begins his long journey back toward life. However, the past is never completely consumed; the ashes always remain. Wiesel's next two novels are different expressions of a healing process in which the author comes to terms with his human entanglements and his duel with God. The partiality of this healing process, however, continues to highlight the void. Wiesel is a twice-born soul who forever affirms the gap between what he once was and what he later became. With the affirmation of life expressed by the rage against death, the long journey back from the kingdom of night begins, a journey back to the world of the living.

Suffering

In *The Town Beyond the Wall* Wiesel comes to terms with the possible meaning of suffering, and on the level of theodicy he expresses compassion for God's predicament. The setting of the novel is a prison in the city of Szerencseváros, the Hungarian town in which Michael, the central character of the novel, was born and raised prior to his adolescence in the concentration camp. Several years after his liberation, Michael decides to return to his place of birth and to confront the townspeople who had been indifferent to his fate. For Wiesel, the imaginary return in *The Town Beyond the Wall* served as a model for his actual return to Sighet in 1964, less than one·year after the publication of the novel.[1] In a sense, both journeys back to childhood were the same. Both underscored Wiesel's distance from the past and the impossibility of return. Both forced him to confront additional devastations to the city of his dreams, and both were cruelly therapeutic.

Throughout his novels Wiesel writes of suffering. He usually emphasizes the internal pain generated by external conditions. His descriptions of pain are evocative. He demands that the reader share his pain and experience the intensity of his suffering. Yet, throughout his early novels, Wiesel maintains that suffering is without any positive value. He does not choose to speak of the lessons that one can learn from suffering and the peculiar virtues of compassion and depth that some people maintain are brought to consciousness only through pain. On the contrary, Wiesel rejects all claims that attribute some positive value to suffering. I have already mentioned the narrator's realization in *Le Jour* that suffering not only changes the victim but can also destroy others. Similarly, in *Le Jour*, Wiesel writes of the fact that man cannot accept the innocent suffering of others for it forces him to confront "the great vacuum . . . at the end of all adventures."[2] Wiesel's most bitter comment on suffering is directed at those who wish

1. Elie Wiesel, *Legends of Our Time* (New York: Avon Books, 1968), pp. 143–163.
2. *The Accident*, p. 106.

to maintain the saintliness of those who suffer. His experience at Auschwitz convinced him otherwise, and he insists that we fully face the implications of that experience. Wiesel can in no way be considered a religious masochist.

"Suffering brings out the lowest, the most cowardly in man. There is a phase of suffering you reach beyond which you become a brute. Beyond it you sell your soul — and worse, the souls of your friends — for a piece of bread, for some warmth, for a moment of oblivion . . . saints are those who die before the end of the story. The others . . . no longer dare look at themselves in the mirror, afraid they may see their inner image . . ."[3]

Perhaps no person can survive the cross and still remain unblemished. For Wiesel, the sainthood of Jesus is directly related to the speed of his death and the fact that he had no opportunity to elaborate on his cry, "My God, my God, why hast Thou forsaken me?"[4]

The redemptive meaning of Michael's suffering in *The Town Beyond the Wall* only underscores the contrasting lack of meaning in the suffering of the concentration camp victims. Wiesel knows that sometimes suffering is of instrumental value. The suffering of Michael was necessary in order for his friend Pedro to survive, and this redemptive meaning remained Michael's constant companion throughout his ordeal. It allowed him to survive with both his integrity and his sanity intact.

Although Wiesel knows that the theodicy of Israel could be preserved if the sufferings of the victims were considered redemptive, he deliberately refuses to grant them a redemptive status. This refusal is but another indication of Wiesel's fidelity to his own experience even at the expense of the theodicy of Israel. Some critics have

3. *Ibid.*, p. 49.
4. *Mark* 15:34.

mistakenly attributed to Wiesel the idea that suffering has a redemptive aspect. Professor Byron Sherwin, in a 1970 article in *Judaism,* made the following claim concerning Wiesel's writings:

. . . The meaning of suffering is to prevent more suffering. The goal of suffering is to ennoble.

Israel waits to whisper the secret of suffering, and the secret of survival to mankind. In the face of nuclear holocaust, the suffering of Israel may be a beacon-light to warn mankind of the price of indifference . . . . The flames of the crematoria do have a purpose; they are a light to the nations.[5]

Sherwin's vision is not without its power for it assigns a Christ-like role to the victims of the Holocaust. It also fulfills certain psychological needs (as will be discussed later). According to Sherwin, the death of the victims will redeem humanity from its own inner tendencies toward self-destruction. Their death renewed Israel's mission to the world. Israel became again the center of civilization with the fate of the world dependent upon her. Once again Israel was charged to reveal the Torah to mankind.

Wiesel does reaffirm the centrality of Israel, but certainly not in the manner suggested by Prof. Sherwin. (Consideration of Wiesel's doctrine of Israel will be deferred until a later chapter.) Professor Sherwin has misread Wiesel by ignoring both the caution in Wiesel's positive statements and the strength of his negative remarks. Professor Sherwin has cited Wiesel's contribution to a symposium on Jewish values in the post-Holocaust future in which Wiesel said the following:

5. Byron L. Sherwin, "Elie Wiesel and Jewish Theology," *Judaism,* Vol. 18, No. 1 (Winter 1969), p. 52.

About Vietnam. Of course, chronologically, Hiroshima follows Auschwitz. Of course, Vietnam takes place in the post-Auschwitz era. Whether we want it or not the Holocaust affected all subsequent events. *Vietnam was made possible, because of what the world did to us in Auschwitz. If mankind is to be destroyed, it will be a result of Auschwitz.* If there is a lesson to be found in Auschwitz it is for the world to learn, not for us . . . The world should learn its own lesson on its own level for its own good, namely: when people do things of this nature to Jews, tomorrow they will do them to themselves. This, perhaps, may be our mission to the world: we are to save it from self-destruction. . . . By now it [the world] must admit that we have in our possession a key to survival. We have not survived centuries of atrocities for nothing.

This is what I think we are trying to prove to ourselves, desperately . . . . We must invent reason; we must create beauty out of nothingness . . .

This is not a lesson; this is not an answer. It is only a question.[6] (italics mine)

Wiesel's statement has been quoted at length not only in order to avoid confusion but to illustrate specifically where and how Wiesel can be misread unless his remarks are considered fully and contextually. To imply an ennobling character to suffering is to fly in the face of all that Wiesel has previously said about suffering. To understand this quote as a positive, affirmative statement not merely of the meaning but of the *purpose* of the crematoria goes against all of the cautionary words that Wiesel included in this paragraph. Wiesel said: "*perhaps,* this is our mission," or "*if* there is a lesson." He spoke of the positive not as a lesson or an answer but as a question, a struggle, a battle

6. Elie Wiesel, "On Jewish Values in the Post-Holocaust Future," *Judaism,* Vol. 16, No. 3 (Summer 1967), p. 299.

to affirm something in the face of nothingness. Purpose implies intent prior to the act. Who is it that gave this purpose to the crematoria and what can we say of him?

Furthermore, Professor Sherwin has confused his claim that the victims serve as a beacon of light with Wiesel's claim that the perpetrators of the crimes of Auschwitz have established a precedent that has raised the world's tolerance level for inhumanity. In reality, the victims have died and the world has remained indifferent to other tragedies, including Jewish tragedies. Other atrocities have been allowed. Wiesel wrote in *One Generation After*:

> . . . the failure of the black years has begotten yet another failure. Nothing has been learned; *Auschwitz has not even served as warning*. For more detailed information, consult your daily newspaper.[7] (italics mine)

Where is the beacon of light and how has it illuminated the second half of the twentieth century? Even if Sherwin were correct and the purpose of the crematoria were to enable Israel to be a light unto the nations, reality demands that we recognize the vacuity of the sacrifice, the failure of the light.[8] The messiahs have died, and the world has not been redeemed. The flames of the crematoria did not produce light; they produced a thick, black smoke. They consumed the living and gave back only ashes.

7. Elie Wiesel, *One Generation After* (New York: Avon Books, 1970), p. 15.

8. Perhaps Sherwin's most persuasive argument could be drawn from the way the Israelis and the American Blacks have used Jewish behavior in the Holocaust as the perfect example of how *not* to behave. Is this the purpose that Sherwin intends? For a discussion of the Israeli attitude toward the Holocaust see Saul Esh, "The Dignity of the Destroyed: Toward a Definition of the Period of the Holocaust," *Judaism*, Vol. 15, No. 1 (Spring 1962). Most Americans are familiar with the Blacks' contention that 'we refuse to behave like Jews.' This argument, which has some degree of cogency, is far different from the one Sherwin advances.

Professor Sherwin has not only misread the intent of the passage he cites from Wiesel but has also failed to consider the numerous times Wiesel has stated without qualification that the Holocaust has no meaning. It defies meaning. The Holocaust marks "the defeat of the intellect that wants to find a Meaning — with a capital M — in history."[9] Wiesel has even rejected the claim that the foundation of the state of Israel offers some redemptive meaning to the sacrifice of the concentration camp victims.

Israel, an answer to the holocaust? It is too convenient, too scandalous a solution. First, because it would impose a burden, an unwarranted guilt feeling, on our children. To pretend that without Auschwitz there would be no Israel is to endow the latter with a share of responsibility for the former. And second, Israel cannot be an answer to the holocaust, because the holocaust, by its very magnitude, by its essence too, negates all answers.[10]

The scandal of the attempt to treat Israel as the redemptive factor for the Holocaust is that the executioner arrives before the Messiah. Israel was founded after the Holocaust and could not undo the horror of the death camps. Even if the traditional Messiah were to appear now, his presence would come too late to save those who had so urgently awaited his arrival.

Friendship and the Possibility of Meaning

If suffering is redemptive, it is so only in the human domain. One may give to another, suffer pain for another, and endure torture so that another may live. Friendship entails some pain and some sacrifice. Toward the end of *Le Jour* the correspondent began to learn about friendship.

9. *Legends of Our Time*, pp. 223–224.
10. *One Generation After*, p. 166.

It was Gyula, the artist friend of Eliezer, and to a lesser extent Kathleen, his lover, who brought him back from the brink of death. It was Gyula whose friendship demanded from him a staunch self-confidence. Success in friendship as well as in teaching hinges on the issue of interdependence as opposed to dependence or independence. Complete dependence, as was the case with Kathleen, destroys both the friends and the friendship. At the other extreme, complete independence prevents real interaction. Gyula, for example, was unqualified as a master for he sought to protect his strength and preserve his own independence. Only a measure of interdependence can evoke the depths of learning and love. Pedro's relationship with Michael in *The Town Beyond the Wall* is a good example of such a relationship. Pedro's own power and inner congruity allowed him to explore with Michael the realms of interdependence.

It is interesting to note that throughout his novels Wiesel repeatedly depicts a master who instructs his characters in the mysteries of the depths. In *A Beggar in Jerusalem* Kalman was the master in the realm of the divine mysteries. In *Dawn* the old man taught Elisha the secrets of battle and history. In *Legends of Our Time* and *One Generation After* the Wandering Jew instructed Wiesel in all the domains of depth. In *The Town Beyond the Wall* Pedro's task was to instruct Michael in the mysteries of friendship.

Pedro represents the beginning of Michael's reconciliation with suffering, finitude, and friendship. Pedro is unique among the characters in Wiesel's novels for while he shares the depth of all of Wiesel's main characters, he neither shares their memory of the camps nor their Jewish memories. His memories are of Spain and of a civil war in which even the dead were raped. He is a character of unusual power and profound insight. He prays for the power to sin against God and to oppose His will. He is aware of the dialectical nature of the relationship between man and God, a dialectic that yields no resolution. God, he says, "is the weakness of strong men and the strength of weak men. . . . Man is God's strength. Also His weakness."[11] For Pedro the human drama is not one of exile and return or union and separation, but one of simplicity and complexity. The fall marked the end of simplicity. For Pedro, love and death are intimately connected. We love unto death. We get hurt. We risk and try to love again.

Pedro spoke with Michael of their differences and of their divergent views toward the persistence of evil. Pedro said:

> You frighten me. . . . You want to eliminate suffering by pushing it to its extreme: to madness. To say 'I suffer, therefore I am' is to become the enemy of man. What you must say is 'I suffer, therefore you are.' Camus wrote somewhere that to protest against a universe of unhappiness you had to create happiness. That's an arrow pointing the way: it leads to another human being. And not via absurdity.[12]

These are the words that Michael found most helpful in life. The Spaniard wanted to live in the face of evil and to create in the face of finitude. Michael, the Jew, wanted to eradicate evil and to create that which would endure for eternity. The Jew had much to learn from the Spaniard.

Pedro also instructed Michael in the nature of the cosmic struggle that gave rise to this response. Michael had spoken of the death of a young child who had become old before his time and of his own reaction to that death. He

11. Elie Wiesel, *The Town Beyond the Wall* (New York: Holt, Rinehart & Winston, 1964), p. 9.
12. *Ibid.,* p. 118.

expressed this reaction simply in the prayer, "Oh, God! Make me be silence! Make me be! Be . . ."[13] Michael yearned to leave the world of becoming and the world of flux, to endure, timeless, unchanging, untouched, and unhurt. Pedro responded, and Wiesel describes the scene as a moment of revelation in which "Pedro was no longer a body, but a voice. His whole being reposed in his voice."[14]

"It's the divine will . . . that if·a man has something to say, he says it most perfectly by taking unto him a woman and creating a new man. And then God remembers that he too has something to say; and he entrusts the message to the Angel of Death. But even so, your creation isn't a total loss. Something of it persists. A question, and that's a lot. Suddenly you become aware of the agony of living, of seeing loneliness, of seeing pain, of seeing agony. The dialogue — or the duel, if you like — between man and his God doesn't end in nothingness. Man may not have the last word, but he has the last cry. That moment marks the birth of art."

"And of friendship," I said.

"Friendship is an art."[15]

For Pedro life is a duel between man and God. Man seeks to create and to build, and God reminds all creation of its finitude. Like Roqueuntin in Sartre's *Nausea*, Pedro sees that art may endure but only as a challenge or a question in the face of an all-consuming absurdity. As we shall see, Wiesel retains this insight and clothes it in a Jewish idiom and in a Jewish protagonist in his later works *The Oath* and *Zalmen, or the Madness of God*.

13. *Ibid.*, p. 95.
14. *Ibid.*, p. 96.
15. *Ibid.*, p. 96.

In the *Town Beyond the Wall* Michael applies Pedro's lessons to his own prison situation and in the process discovers the possibility of meaning in living for another and in helping the other. In prison he discovers that meaning can be found in giving and in creating and that by healing another one can help heal oneself. Wiesel affirms the possibility of meaning in the face of nothingness, but it is a new type of meaning. This affirmation provides a measure of reconciliation for Wiesel's protagonist and serves as a fragmentary response, a respite in his effort to understand the mysteries of human existence.

In prison Michael assumes the role that Pedro would want for him. As God is a consolation for Menachem,[16] a fellow inmate of Michael's, so Pedro is Michael's consolation and Michael's strength. God no longer plays that role for Michael. In working with the young boy, his withdrawn celimate, and seeking to cure him, Michael is duplicating the creation of the universe by creating order out of chaos. When Michael speaks to the young boy, the voice that echoes within him is the voice of Pedro. The wisdom of the Spaniard becomes the message of the Jew.

"I know, little one: it isn't easy to live always under a question mark. But who says that the essential question has an answer? The essence of man is to be a question, and the essence of the question is to be without answer.

Man has the right to risk life, his own life; he does not need to submerge himself in destiny in order to maintain his deep significance. He must risk, he can risk a confrontation with destiny, he must try to seize what he demands, to ask the great questions and ask them again . . ."[17]

16. Again the importance of names must be stressed since Menachem in Hebrew means to console.
17. *Ibid.*, pp. 176–177.

Michael admonishes the young boy never to abandon humanity but to remember that remaining human involves a risk in a world that offers little security. One must affirm and create in the face of impending nothingness. As in *Dawn,* Wiesel rejects the Jew's dependence upon God for redemption. He also further narrows the need for ontological support for human creativity and meaning.

Images of God in Wiesel's Writings

When we consider the images of God in the writings of Elie Wiesel, the continuity between Wiesel and past Jewish tradition becomes noticeable as do the discontinuities. There have been two tendencies within Jewish theology: the one is to construct systems and recite dogma; the other is to tell tales and to have the telling of tales serve as the form for doing theology. The former mode of reflecting upon Jewish religious experience was prevalent throughout the middle ages in the rationalist schools and in the nineteenth- and twentieth-century schools of Jewish philosophy, while the latter process found its paramount expression in Rabbinic Midrash and Hasidic tales. Elie Wiesel has continued in this tradition of developing theology through tales.

Three general observations about the nature of Wiesel's midrash should be made. Firstly, Wiesel depicts the Holocaust not merely as an event within his biography or within history but as a communal event that must be absorbed into the totality of Jewish history. Memory for Wiesel is not exclusively his individual memory but the collective memory of a people. He both shares his own memory and absorbs the group memory as his own. Secondly, Wiesel's symbolic language, his cultural community and his mythic universe, are direct continuities of Midrashic, Kabbalistic, and Hasidic Judaism. Nevertheless, what is distinct about the man as an artist and what is most revelatory of his theological position is not what he has taken from the tradition but what he has transformed in the tradition. In Wiesel's work the traditional forms have been accepted and preserved while their content has been transformed. I shall return to this point again and again in my analysis of Wiesel's images. Thirdly, since Wiesel is most manifestly acquainted with the original sources, we must assume that where he distorts or transforms the original images such a transformation is deliberate. We may not assume that the transformation or distortion is based on ignorance or done without foreknowledge.

As Wiesel moves away from the traditional theodicy of Israel, the metaphors that he uses to speak of God also shift. They become a bit less harsh and far more empathetic in reference to the divine predicament. In his early novels Wiesel continually searched for the proper image with which to capture the horror of an indifferent universe. In *Dawn* when Elisha goes downstairs to meet his victim, he discovers a man rather than an abstract enemy. He comments: "The lack of hate between executioner and victim, perhaps this is God."[18] In *Le Jour* we have already seen some of the images that Wiesel uses to speak of God. Man is God's favorite toy, His amusement; he is the manner by which God seeks to relieve himself of solitary boredom. At another point in *Le Jour* Wiesel employs the ugliest image of God. The correspondent recalls an instance in which he met a prostitute whose name was Sarah.[19] Sarah was a young girl when she was taken to the concentration camp, and she was used as a sexual object

18. *Dawn,* p. 76.
19. Sarah was also the name of Wiesel's mother as well as the name of the matriarch of the Jewish people.

for the entertainment of the S.S. officers. Now an old woman of sixteen, she thinks of herself as unattractive, for men do not want to make love to one who is no longer twelve. Struck by the horror of the situation, the corre-spondent recalls the verse from *Exodus* in which God said, "For man shall not see me and live."[20] Wiesel gives the verse a new and profoundly horrible meaning. "Why can't man see God and live? Because God is ashamed, deeply ashamed, that He likes to sleep with twelve-year-old girls."[21] Wiesel uses this horrible and absurd explanation of God to capture his own sense of existential horror.

At another point in *Le Jour* Wiesel again comments on the Biblical verse. At this point his image is far less harsh although it is still quite powerful.

"You can love God, but you can't look at Him."

"Whom do you look at when you love God?" she asked after a moment of silence.

"Yourself. If man could contemplate the face of God, he would stop loving Him. God needs love; He does not need understand-ing."[22]

To come face to face with God and still love Him is not humanly possible. Even Moses could only see His other side.

In *Night* Wiesel employs a number of painful images to

20. *Exodus* 34:20.
21. *Le Jour,* p. 93.
22. *Ibid.,* p. 11. Wiesel is fascinated by this Biblical verse and reinterprets it over and over again. For example, in *A Beggar in Jerusalem* he writes:

> Over there, in the camp, a wise and pious inmate had cried out in a fit of madness: "All of us heard God in the desert; here we shall be allowed to see Him." —— "Yes," the others had answered, "we shall see Him and perish." The image of God cannot be transmit-ted; it can be carried away only in death. (p. 100)

speak of God. He compares God unfavorably to Hitler, claiming that Hitler at least kept his promise to the Jewish people. He describes a young boy who was loved by his fellow inmates as a sad-eyed angel, a child with a beautiful and refined face. Sentenced to die by hanging, the boy is too light to die and too brave to implicate others in his conspiracy. Wiesel writes:

> For more than half an hour he stayed there, struggling between life and death, dying in slow agony under our eyes . . .
>
> Behind me I heard the same man asking: "Where is God now?"
>
> And I heard a voice within me answer him: "Where is He? Here He is, hanging here on this gallows . . ."[23]

God dies when the innocent and the young die. The belief in God is killed in the human mind when the slaughter of innocence destroys the credibility of a just world. God is implicated in the death of the innocent, or perhaps God, in his omnipotent impotence, struggles between life and death. Perhaps He too can neither shout nor die.

These images should not be taken literally or systematically, but they should be taken evocatively. Wiesel continues a long tradition within Jewish theology of dealing with the images of God in order to satisfy an existential need. His images are suggestive and, as his existential needs change, the character of his images changes.

In *The Town Beyond the Wall* Wiesel speaks far less of God than in *Night*. However, when he does speak of God, the images he employs suggest a shift in perspective. Michael's imprisonment generates a new understanding of God.

In prison, under torture, man becomes powerful, omnipotent.

23. *Night*, p. 76.

He becomes God. That's the secret: God is imprisoned! . . .
Man must free him. That is the best-guarded secret since the
creation.[24]

The image of an imprisoned God is not suggested by
Wiesel in the Kabbalistic sense in which man's task is to
unify and thus free God. Rather, Wiesel is pointing toward
the paradox of inner strength and outer impotence, of
having power over others, while having no power to de-
termine one's own fate.

The Omnipotence of Man as a Response to God

Throughout *The Town Beyond the Wall* Wiesel is fascinated by man's ability to combat God and to impose his
will upon the universe. As has been stated, Michael means
in Hebrew "who is like God." This is an important question for Wiesel, and he answers it although he knows that
any answer to the question other than "there is no one like
God" is heretical. Wiesel answers the question with the
claim that man is like God. Wiesel insists that man must be
like God. Man must impose his will upon the universe,
upon God. While in the beginning Michael prayed for the
strength to remain faithful to God, he later altered his
prayer to coincide with the prayer of Pedro's madman:
". . . give me the strength to sin against you, to oppose your
will! Give me the strength to deny you, to reject you, to
imprison you, ridicule you!"[25] The human quest for omnipotence is madness and destined to failure. Nevertheless, Wiesel loves people most when they strive for omnipotence and when they are strong enough to force their
will upon the universe.

Wiesel's early religious stance as he recalls it to us also

24. *The Town Beyond the Wall*, p. 10.
25. *Ibid.*, p. 48.

exhibits a great fascination with the power of the individual and the quest for omnipotence. He recalls an early warning by his grandfather.

You must not copy the Rebbe's gestures, you are not to imitate him again. You can follow and obey him, but that's all. Don't try to assume his role; one does not reach for the royal scepter with impunity. Even if the king appears to be absent.[26]

Wiesel also tells us of his attempts at self-mortification and prayer and of the fellowship he joined in order to force God to send the Messiah. Jewish legend abounds in tales of those who sought to force God's hand and almost succeeded, only to meet failure in the end.[27] Wiesel knows these tales. He repeats them over and over again.[28] Nevertheless, as a youngster, Wiesel joined a group of three in devout resolution to force God to send his Messiah, and this group vowed to succeed where all others had failed before them. This stance of religious arrogance borders on blasphemy, but both the young Wiesel and the older Wiesel wholeheartedly support it.

26. *One Generation After*, p. 25.
27. An early example of this occurring in Jewish legend is found in *Sanhedrin* 97b.
28. Wiesel relates the following tale:

A famous medieval cabalist, Joseph di-la Reina, made up his mind to put an end to the comedy which man is condemned to play against himself and to bring about the advent of the Messiah. At the cost of considerable sacrifice the great sage overcame Satan and threw him into chains. Everywhere — in heaven and upon earth, in paradise and in Hell — there was a great commotion: the end was at hand. But the sage made one mistake: he took pity on his captive and succumbed to his tears. Pity is a double-edged weapon, and Satan knows how to use it. He broke his chains, and the Messiah, already on the threshold, was forced to return to his prison, somewhere infinitely far away, in the chaos of time and man's hope. Everything had to start all over, because the poor miracle-maker had a heart which wasn't hard enough. (*The Gates of the Forest*, p. 18.)

Wiesel continues to be fascinated by man's quest for omnipotence. This desire for omnipotence may be one of the roots of his attraction to the legends of the *Zaddik,* the righteous leader of the Hasidic community. The Zaddik, in the eyes of his followers, had certain awesome powers. He could traverse distances without being subject to the limitations of space and time. He could heal the sick merely by imposing his will upon the course of the universe. He could make fertile the barren by·the strength of his will. As Wiesel describes him:

> With a single look he could destroy buildings and raise them up again. With a word he could deny the power of fate and substitute his own for it. *Hatzadik gozer vehakadosh baruch hu mekayem,* says the Talmud. The righteous decree and the Holy One, blessed be He, obeys.[29]

The Zaddik is an all-knowing, all-powerful individual, the concrete embodiment of the human desire for omnipotence and therefore a figure of genuine appeal for his politically impotent followers. Wiesel hints at the roots of this appeal when he writes:

> They needed to believe that God took an interest in His creation, that He listened to all the voices; they needed to believe that miracles were still possible, even for them.[30]

But at Auschwitz the Zaddik did not perform the expected miracles. His powers were either not exercised or they proved ineffective. His omnipotence proved impotent in a world of death, for "death negates miracles, the death of 1,000,000 children negates more than miracles."[31] Wiesel was forced to reject the Zaddik's omnipotence, but he

29. *The Gates of the Forest,* p. 190.
30. Elie Wiesel, *Souls on Fire* (New York: Random House, 1972), p. 35.
31. *Ibid.,* p. 37.

continued to search for the sense in which the individual could be omnipotent.

In *The Town Beyond the Wall* Wiesel develops the character of Varady, a heretical genius who believed passionately in the omnipotence of man. Varady was a young and gifted student in Michael's home town. He was considered an *illui,* a prodigy, and was ordained at fifteen years of age. For three years prior to his twenty-second birthday, he stayed in absolute seclusion studying the mysteries of the Kabbalah and trying to discern the secrets of existence. At the end of these three years, he addressed the congregation and revealed his determination to defy death, to defy God, and to live forever. Varady emphasized the strength of man who could bring the Messiah.

He claimed that liberation from Time would be accomplished at the signal of man, and not of his Creator; the irony and beauty of it was that "each of you, the men and women who hear me, has God in his power, for each of you is capable of achieving a thing of which God is incapable! . . . *Man is not what he does, but what he wishes!* He will conquer heaven, earth, sickness, and death if he will only raze the walls that imprison the Will. And I who speak to you announce here solemnly my decision to deny death, to repel it, to ridicule it! He who stands before you will never die!"[32] (italics mine)

Varady was forced from the community, and he wandered throughout the world visiting monasteries and Ashrams, living in the city and in the country, sojourning among friends, and living alone. For Wiesel there are two additional dimensions to the legend of Varady. He survived his peers and lived through succeeding generations until finally, under the Nazis, his reign of immortality came to an end. Varady, however, did have the opportunity to

32. *The Town Beyond the Wall,* p. 32.

choose his own death and to insure that the fact of his death would remain concealed. Secondly, despite his heretical beliefs, Varady never denied his people. Although he denied God, he refused to deny the Jewish people. Wiesel approves of this kind of heresy, the heresy from within.

From Varady Michael learned to love the strength of man, to detest weakness and cowardice, and to accept the hatred that comes to one who "shook the ramparts that defended their cowardice."[33] Michael also learned to demand more of himself, not to give in and not to yield to his own inner weakness. These lessons served Michael well in prison as he attempted to recreate the universe. They were also partially responsible for his arrest. Michael was arrested precisely because he challenged the cowardice of the indifferent and because he demanded action from those who preferred to remain bystanders to the events of history. The lessons that Michael learned from Varady formed the root of Michael's response to Job. Since Wiesel has been called 'the Job of Auschwitz' and since many critics tend to view his writings as a contemporary expression of a Jobian view,[34] it is critical that we consider Michael's remarks on Job.

33. *Ibid.,* p. 28.
34. Maurice Friedman explored the parallels between Job and Wiesel in *To Deny Our Nothingness* (New York: Delacorte Press, 1967), pp. 348–353. He is correct in his assertion that Wiesel does identify with Job. Wiesel wrote in *Legends of Our Time:*

. . . I prefer to take my place on the side of Job, who chose questions and not answers, silence and not speeches. (p. 221)

The early Wiesel was far more antagonistic toward Job and less tolerant of his yielding. This may partially be due to Wiesel's failure to reinterpret Job in his early writings and to the reinterpretation that he gives to Job and other challengers to God in his later writings. An example of this shift in attitude is to be found in *Souls on Fire* where Wiesel, in speaking of Rabbi Levi Yitzchak of Berditchev, said of his attacks on God:

Michael never ceased resenting Job. That Biblical rebel should never have given in. At the last moment he should have reared up, shaken a fist, and with a resounding bellow defied that transcendent, inhuman justice in which suffering has no weight in the balance.[35]

Michael felt that he must oppose God. He must refuse to be intimidated by God. Man must refuse to yield. He must pit his strength against God. The power of protest must be equal to the voice from the whirlwind and, in the end, protest must emerge. Wiesel's attitude toward Job as expressed in his first four novels must be considered in light of Michael's remarks. His disappointment with Job is intimately connected with his own fascination with omnipotence, an omnipotence that demands that man resist.

In his chapter on Job in *Messengers of God* Wiesel states that he is most pleased with the Job who is powerful and refuses to yield. He is disappointed in the final image of the weak Job, a "broken, defeated man. On his knees, having surrendered unconditionally. God magnanimously allowed him to stand up again. And live again."[36]

Wiesel writes that he admires Job's passionate rebellion but is troubled by his hasty abdication. He prefers to think that the true ending of the tale has been lost. Perhaps Friedman's claim that Wiesel is the Job of Auschwitz should be remembered in terms of the unreconciled Job, the rebellious man who refused to surrender. If this be the case, then the alternate ending to Job's tale is one we must construct.

As a child I loved them and saw in them nothing but love and friendship. Today I feel their weight of despair and revolt and love them even more. (p. 91)

35. *The Town Beyond the Wall*, p. 52.
36. *Messengers of God*, p. 232.

Chapter Three

The Gates of the Forest: *The Partial Reconciliation with the Traditions of Israel*

IN *The Gates of the Forest* Wiesel modifies his stance on omnipotence as he becomes reconciled with weakness and cowardice. The protagonist of the book returns to the world of Wiesel's early childhood. This return home to the world of the spirit is no less significant than Michael's geographical return to the Hungarian town of his youth in *The Town Beyond the Wall.* The spiritual return is just as healing as the physical return although it reveals an ontological void. In *The Gates of the Forest* Wiesel comes to terms with the traditions of the past and, in a limited way, reappropriates them for the future. However, this reappropriation does not presume the validity of the sacred theodicy of normative Judaism. On the contrary, it is through the rejection of that theodicy that Wiesel's protagonist begins to live again and to reconstruct his life with a certain fidelity and peace. In *The Gates of the Forest* a heretic returns home to experience a sense of both strangeness and belonging, and thus comes to terms with his past.

Gregor's journey home differs from the journey of all the other central characters in Wiesel's novels. Gregor did

not experience the world of the camps and the memory of
that type of inhumanity. But he did share with Wiesel's other
characters the experience of expulsion, the wealth of a
strong Jewish background, the teachings of the Kabbala,
and the desire to confront God in order to vindicate humanity. Gregor's world was the world of the partisans, a
world of fighters. His world was also a world of hiding and
running and a world in which all that was sacred went up
in smoke to join the clouds. Wiesel forces Gregor to hear
from a friend and thus reconstruct in his mind the horror
that resembles the childhood experiences of Elisha,
Michael, and of Wiesel himself. Of Haimi, Gregor thought:

Poor boy! . . . Our solitude will never equal yours. You know
already that the heart of man is only a cemetery; the more open
it becomes, the greater is the cold. At your age a loss opens a
deeper wound, takes on a more total meaning than treachery. If
your father is dead, it means that God is unjust, that life is a
farce. It means that God doesn't love man or deserve his love.
That fact is the stumbling-block on which he will build his idea
of the world. In the beginning God created man in order to kill
him; he created him because he has no pity.[1]

The similarity between Gregor's thought and Wiesel's
reality is apparent in this passage although in the first three
sections of the novel the author took pains to separate
these two realities. In the end, with the return to the world
of Hasidism, Gregor's world and Wiesel's become one.
The date and manner of Gregor's father's death and his
attitude toward the anniversary of his father's death resemble in all significant details Wiesel's description of the
death of his father in *Legends of Our Time*.[2] Although the
author and his character arrive in Williamsburg, Brooklyn

1. *The Gates of the Forest*, p. 134.
2. *Legends of Our Time*, pp. 15–21.

(the home of many Hasidic communities) by disparate routes and depart to different worlds, they visit the same Hasidic community.

In *The Gates of the Forest* Wiesel resolves his questions concerning both love and faith. His return to the world of the faithful cannot be understood as a complete reconciliation with either God or the traditions that viewed God and humanity in harmony. There can be no complete reconciliation, but there can be a *détente*. It is possible to come to terms with the past in a way that allows one to live in the present and to build for the future. Most critics emphasize the reconciliation with the past that is found in *The Gates of the Forest*.[3] Gregor does return to the synagogue. He is transformed by the singing and the dancing. He finds the presence of his past community consoling. He envies both their faith and their fervor. He does readopt his Jewish name, Gavriel (in Hebrew, 'man of God') which he had previously given away to a nameless companion who joined him in the cave. He does join the Yeshiva boy in prayer. He does return home to face the task of rebuilding his life with Clara, his wife and the former mistress of his companion-in-arms, and he takes home the phylacteries. Above all, he does recite the Kaddish, the prayer for the dead which affirms God's goodness and which Eliezer found impossible to recite when his faith was shattered in *Night*.[4]

The critics' case for a reconciliation with the past is persuasive. Thomas Indinopulos claims that Wiesel comes

3. See Byron Sherwin, "Elie Wiesel and Jewish Theology," *Judaism*, Vol. 18, No. 1 (Winter 1969), or Thomas Idinopulos, "The Holocaust in the Stories of Elie Wiesel," *Soundings*, Vol. 55, No. 2 (Summer 1972), or Irving Halpern, *Messengers from the Dead* (Philadelphia: Westminster Press, 1970).

4. *Night*, p. 43.

to know again "that God is, and that it is possible to live without hating Him."[5] Irving Halpern contends that "the Jobian survivor chooses to speak to Him [God] and to wait for a response."[6] According to these critics, *The Gates of the Forest* marks a reconciliation with God and an acceptance of His world. I would argue that the reconciliation that Wiesel expresses applies to an acceptance of life in the face of the void rather than to an acceptance of God and His universe. Wiesel does not return to the sacred theodicy of Israel. Rather, he returns to the ways of the Jewish people in order to grapple with meaninglessness.

There are three critical points that must be considered in order to understand the final section of *The Gates of the Forest*. The first point relates to Gregor's discussion with the Rebbe. Gregor, the central character of the novel, entered into a dialogue with the Rebbe, the righteous leader of the Hasidic community. Wiesel takes pains to underscore the fact that this is a dialogue between a deserter and a faithful master. Both the Rebbe and Gregor sought victory in their dialogue. Gregor wanted the Rebbe to cry out and to use his awesome spiritual powers in order to alter the world and to force God's hand. The Rebbe wanted to remain aloof from the confrontation, immune to the arguments that Gregor had advanced. He wanted to maintain his role as a Rebbe, a faithful counselor to a man desperately in need. Gregor and the Rebbe both attained their victories although neither man enjoyed them. It is highly significant that Gregor forced the Rebbe to cry out. He forced the Rebbe to acknowledge the validity of his position. Prior to yielding, the Rebbe offered a series of responses to Gregor, responses which clearly

5. Indinopulos, p. 214.
6. Halpern, p. 103.

resemble the ways in which the Hasidic community has confronted the Holocaust.[7]

None of these responses satisfied Gregor either existentially or theologically. He continued to confront the Rebbe. Finally, the Rebbe yielded, but he yielded with a question:

> He's guilty; do you think I don't know it? That I have no eyes to see, no ears to hear? . . . Yes, he [God] is guilty. He has become the ally of evil, of death, of murder, but the problem is still not solved. I ask you a question and dare you answer: 'What is there left for us to do?'[8]

This is the question that Gregor has been asking. It is also the question of Michael, Elisha, and Eliezer. How does one live in a world in which the future ''is mortgaged from the first day, from the first cry''?[9]

The tentative answer that both the Rebbe and Gregor

---

7. The best English-language collection of Hasidic responses to the Holocaust is to be found in Peter Schlindler's informative but inadequate doctoral dissertation *Responses of Hasidic Leaders and Hasidim during the Holocaust* (New York University, 1972). Schlindler's collection of Hasidic responses is flawed by his failure to treat them systematically. Another recent work also probes the ethical as well as the theological responses of orthodox Jewry to the Holocaust, namely Irving Rosenbaum's *The Holocaust and Halakhah* (New York: Ktav Publishing House, 1976).

Jerome Mintz presents an interesting series of ways in which the Hasidic community in its legends has come to terms with the Holocaust. See his work, *Legends of the Hasidim* (Chicago: University of Chicago Press, 1968). The argument that Wiesel presents on the Rebbe's behalf is also instructive. The Rebbe argues:

> Auschwitz proves that nothing has changed, that the primeval war goes on. Man is capable of love and hate, murder and sacrifice. He is Abraham and Isaac together. God Himself hasn't changed. (*The Gates of the Forest*, p. 194.)

We will see this same argument reassert itself in *The Oath*.

8. *The Gates of the Forest*, p. 199.

9. *Ibid.*, p. 221.

give to this question is that in a world devoid of God, one must focus on humanity. Gregor said:

"I owe God nothing. Quite the contrary."

Rebbe: "That's not the question. He owes you nothing either. You don't live his life and he doesn't live yours. You owe yourself something."[10]

What is it that Gregor owed himself? How does one focus on humanity? These are the lessons that Gregor sought to learn from the Hasidic community and from their celebrations.

The second point that is crucial to an understanding of the final scene in *The Gates of the Forest* involves the Rebbe's relationship with the rest of his community. It is critical to note that the Rebbe did not explode the mystery to his followers. They participated in it. The bearer of teachings and his students live in different universes linked only by teaching and faith. For Gregor, however, the mystery of Hasidism had been exploded. Therefore, he inhabited a different world than the followers of the master. He was an observer more than a participant. His observations and discoveries applied to another life outside the community. Gregor could not remain in the Hasidic world even though he had found in it much that enhanced his life.

Gregor discovered that Hasidism is a way of combating despair by sharing it. It is a way of finding hope by living in hope. It is a way of overcoming mourning by demanding joy. The Hasid is one whose rebellion is found in his fidelity. He is a man who cries with song and mourns with joy and who disobeys by remaining obedient. Gregor came to share Marx's analysis of religion and would agree that:

10. *Ibid.*, p. 196.

Religion is the sigh of the oppressed, the heart of a heartless world, just as it is the spirit of a spiritless situation. It is the opiate of the people.[11]

Unlike Marx, who believed that there could be a revolutionary alternative to historical reality, Gregor did not believe that there are any such alternatives. Gregor's world, like the world of Wiesel, is a world without a Messiah and a world in which people may need opiates in order to survive. What is left is man and woman. If meaning is to be found, it is in community and in the love between a man and a woman.

Thirdly, critics differ in their understanding of what is meant by the Kaddish in the final scene of *The Gates of the Forest*. Is Gregor putting the past to rest? Is the Kaddish an expression of faith in God and in His ultimate justice? Is it a Jobian outcry in the face of the whirlwind? Wiesel gives us the clues by which we can interpret the final Kaddish scene. It has already been mentioned that when asked to pray, Gregor recalls his father's death. It should also be noted, as mentioned earlier, that the date and the manner of Gregor's father's death coincide with Wiesel's father's death. In *Legends of Our Time* Wiesel writes of his father's death. He is disturbed by the pending anniversary of his father's death. Had his father lived out his natural years and died a normal death, Wiesel would have known how to commemorate his death. He would have gone to synagogue, led the services, studied the Mishnah, and recited the Kaddish. But his father's death was not normal. To Wiesel it was an outrage. He writes:

. . . on the level of God, it [Auschwitz] will forever remain the most disturbing of mysteries.[12]

11. Karl Marx, "Contribution to a Critique of Hegel's Philosophy of Right," Karl Marx and F. Engels, *On Religion* (New York: Schocken Books, 1959), p. 66.
12. *Legends of Our Time*, p. 20.

God's presence at Treblinka or Maidanek — or, for that matter, his absence — poses a problem which will remain forever insoluble.[13]

Wiesel's conclusions may offer a key for understanding Gregor's recitation of the Kaddish in *The Gates of the Forest*. Wiesel concludes that "By studying the sacred texts, we offer the dead continuity if not peace. It was thus that my father commemorated the death of his father."[14] Wiesel resolves:

> . . . I shall go to the Synagogue after all. I will light the candles, I will say Kaddish, and it will be for me a further proof of my impotence.[15]

Traditions no longer mean what they once did. Nevertheless, they are significant in allowing a person to face his fate. They allow one to reappropriate the past.

Michael, who was proud of his strength and who challenged God by recreating the universe in the face of opposition and imprisonment, has given way to Gavriel who recites the Kaddish for he knows no other way of putting death behind him. Michael was able to stand alone and did not allow God to penetrate the walls of the prison. Gavriel stands in need of community and love in order to survive. The Kaddish which Eliezer refused to say was for Gavriel a dramatization of his accommodation with the past and for Wiesel the way in which man lives with both impotence and omnipotence in the face of God and the universe.

It is clear that there is some measure of reconciliation in *The Gates of the Forest*, but if we accept the notion of the Kaddish as seen in *Legends of Our Time*, if we then

13. *Ibid.*, p. 19.
14. *Ibid.*, p. 20.
15. *Ibid.*, p. 21.

consider the fact that Gregor forces the Rebbe to concede the veracity of his attack on God, and if we also give proper credence to the partial-observer role that Gregor assumes in his stance toward the community, then we must be careful in attributing undue importance to the reconciliation. The best that can be said is that the reconciliation is partial. The past is not eradicated. Life and faith do not return to their previous state. The attacks on Jewish theodicy are still valid. However, the author comes to appreciate anew what has been lost not only in the Holocaust, but in the lives of the survivors.

The Reconciliation of Love

The Gates of the Forest marks a dramatic shift in Wiesel's attitude toward love and in the ability of his major characters to handle that dimension of interpersonal encounter. In *Dawn* the love of Gad and Ilana, the Sabra terrorist and his lover, was important to Elisha, but they were Israelis, their life was uncomplicated, and their virtue was their simplicity. For Elisha, love was complex and it could not be dissociated from death. Catherine, the woman who introduced Elisha to the pleasures of the body, his teacher in the mysteries of sensuality, was an older French girl who was also a concentration camp survivor. Elisha recounts:

She had spoken to me of love because she knew that I was the little boy who had been turned into a prayer and carried up into Heaven. She knew that I had died and come back to earth, dead . . . . She liked making love with little boys who were going to die; she enjoyed the company of those who were obsessed with death.[16]

In *Le Jour* Eliezer's relationship with Kathleen was not

16. *Dawn,* p. 51.

much easier. The strength of their original union was their absence of commitment and their ability to walk away. The proud, strong Kathleen was able to descend to the depths of the correspondent's anguish and to share his living hell. In the process she was destroyed and reduced to a shell of her former self. A relationship that was once without bonds became one that constrained both the correspondent and Kathleen to a world of lies and the persistent need for reassurance. The correspondent said:

She [Kathleen] has too much faith in the power, in the omnipotence of love. Love me and you'll be protected. Love each other and all will be well . . . As for me, love or death. I didn't care.[17]

The correspondent was not free from the bonds of the past. He was unable to live in the present and to affirm another. Kathleen became confused in his mind with his mother and grandmother. Her shawl triggered memories of the past that demanded immediate recognition and that precluded a life in the present. The ghosts of the past were far more demanding than the reality of the present. The present could not compete with the omnipotence of the dead.

In *The Town Beyond the Wall* there is a momentary glimpse of the power of love. Milika, the young girl who had cared for Varady and who had threatened the young and pious Michael with her beauty, meets Michael in the streets of Paris. The narrator recounts:

He was surprised at the void Milika filled in his heart. He had never dreamed that an unexpected meeting with her would comfort him so. The emptiness within him became a fullness. The walls seemed less formidable, less insurmountable. A woman is there, and the world is no longer the same. Suddenly everything *is*. Everything becomes simple, true, possible. I am, you are.

17. *The Accident,* pp. 24–25.

That's enough. It means that man is not alone, that the scattered forces are somewhere reunited.[18]

The reference to the reunion of scattered forces is Lurrianic. It would be a mistake to interpret this reference literally, for Wiesel's tone seems more ironic and far from literal. Michael's glimpse at the possibilities of love is in contrast with the correspondent's experience with Kathleen.

Gregor's relationship with Clara partially resembles both the correspondent's relationship with Kathleen and Michael's affirmation of love. In *The Gates of the Forest* it is Clara and not Gregor who is the prisoner of the past. She is unable to distinguish between her dead lover and her present husband. She, like the correspondent, is unable to free herself from the ghosts of the past and is trapped in a relationship of mutual dependence and destruction with her husband Gregor. Gregor entered into the relationship with Michael's type of affirmation of love. To Clara he said:

. . . there is more of eternity in the instant which unites two people than in the memory of God, more peace in a gaze into a beloved's heart than in the kingdom of heaven.[19]

Love is the transcendent possibility for man. It is man's attempt to achieve meaning and satisfaction in the wake of nothingness. He who stares into the eyes of his beloved and sees hatred and pain is forsaken by God, and he who achieves true union with a woman comes to know the power of God. Despite the tormented nature of his relationship with Clara, Gregor resolves to return and begin again. He is hoping to put the past to rest and to build a

18. *The Town Beyond the Wall*, p. 79.
19. *The Gates of the Forest*, p. 214.

future. It is with the Kaddish that he bids farewell to the past. It is with the Kaddish that he gathers the strength from tradition and community that allows him to return to his world with Clara.

It is critical to note that this affirmation of love comes not at the beginning but at the end of the journey. Wiesel began as a young child seeking cosmic support for his sense of meaning. This support evaporated with the experiences of the camps, and he was never able to reestablish a sense of meaning in any cosmic dimension. He kept narrowing his scope from ontology to history, from history to life, and from life to love. His affirmation of love was not only a positive affirmation of man and woman, of I and thou, but at the same time it was a confession of the narrow domain in which human life can be meaningful. Like the Hasidic Rabbi who began his career vowing to alter the world, Wiesel discovered in the end that one can at best alter oneself and hopefully have some impact on one's closest relationships. Wiesel's affirmation of love is both poetic and beautiful, yet at the same time it is tinged with a sadness, an eternal sadness, the sadness of a cosmic void.

Wiesel's Early Childhood and the Image of the Void

It is my intention not to psychoanalyze either the author or his writings, but rather to suggest that there is some correlation between these love experiences and the way in which Wiesel experienced the absence of God.

Throughout Wiesel's autobiographical writings his mother is depicted as the principal religious influence on his early life. Wiesel consistently describes his father as a humanist, faithful to the traditions of Israel, but more intensely involved with the affairs of men.

But, though he observed tradition, my father was in no way
fanatic. On the contrary, he preached an open spirit toward the
world. . . . He could be found more often in government offices
than in the synagogue — and sometimes, in periods of danger,
even more often than at home.[20]

The image of father and mother corresponds with the parents of the protagonists in all of Wiesel's novels. In *The
Town Beyond the Wall* Michael's father strenuously ob-
jected to his practice of asceticism and his denial of the
body. He wanted his son to be a philosopher, one who
understood the mystery rather than one who participated in
it. In *The Gates of the Forest,* Shlomo (the name of both
Gregor's and Wiesel's father) preached tolerance even toward one who had defied the traditions of Israel. "To a man
who is freeing himself from God you owe particular respect,
because more than others he is accomplishing his destiny."[21]

Throughout all of Wiesel's works the image of the
father is that of a compassionate humanist who is critical
both of extreme piety and of fanaticism.

Wiesel's mother, on the other hand, seems to have
been the principal influence in Wiesel's early religious life.
She wished her son would become a Rabbi rather than a
philosopher. She encouraged his visits to the Hasidic masters and his study with Kalman the Kabbalist. Wiesel
writes:

My mother seemed more devout than he. It was she who
brought me to *heder* to make me a good Jew, loving only the
wisdom and truth to be drawn from the Torah. And it was she

20. *Legends of Our Time,* p. 16. See also *Harry James Cargas in
Conversation with Elie Wiesel* (Paramus: The Paulist Press, 1976), pp.
62–80.
21. *The Gates of the Forest,* p. 24.

who sent me as often as possible to the Rebbe of Wizsnitz to ask his blessing or simply to expose me to his radiance. . . . My mother taught me love of God.[22]

Wiesel's mother's piety was related to her experience with her father, a Hasid who had a profound influence on Wiesel's life.

There are two principal passages in Wiesel's writings that are directly relevant to an understanding of his mother's influence on his image of the void. One of these passages is directly autobiographical and the other is expressed by Michael in *The Town Beyond the Wall*.

Wiesel's relationship with his mother was extremely powerful. His rivalry with his father for her attention was quite sharp. Wiesel vividly depicts this type of attraction and rivalry in many of his works. In *A Beggar in Jerusalem* David's mother is the embodiment of both faith and tragic vision, and David's attraction to her is quite deep. In *The Town Beyond the Wall* Wiesel presents a lucid and poignant description of strong oedipal rivalries. Michael recalls:

I must have been about nine years old. Father had just come back from a trip. . . . He took off his fur-collared overcoat, presented me with my gifts, and disappeared into the other room with Mother, closing the door. I was unhappy . . . . They were abandoning me, excluding me. I left the house for spite and went into the street, into the snow. I wished for death . . . . That same evening I fell sick. Pneumonia. Temperature 104°. For three days I wavered between life and death. Father and Mother never left my bedside. They didn't even go to the store. They didn't go off to lock themselves in their room.[23]

Michael recalls this incident as his first disillusionment, his

22. *Legends of Our Time*, p. 17.
23. *The Town Beyond the Wall*, p. 139.

first desire for extinction. He had refused to accept his father's prerogative and had fought back with the threat of death in order that he not be ignored.

In an autobiographical essay, "The Orphan," Wiesel presents us with another crucial piece of information concerning his relationship with his mother. Wiesel recounts his early experience of leaving home and going to school.

Among the children whom I did not know and did not want to know, I felt myself to be, like each of them . . . the victim of my parents' injustice. I made up countless illnesses so that I could stay home with my mother for just one more day, to hear her say she still loved me, that she was not going to turn me over to strangers.[24]

This passage can be fully understood if we consider the sociological situation of a small *shtetl* community.[25] The burden of religious continuity fell primarily on the male. It was he who was to be educated, and part of his later status in life as well as the status of his family would depend on his religious education. The young boy would remain at home for three to five years and then would be forced to make the abrupt transition from home to school, from the world of his mother to the long (ten-hour days were considered normal), hard, and tedious world of his father. The transition was marked by a ceremony in which the boy was wrapped in a tallit (a prayer shawl) and carried to *Heder* where his first moment of study was celebrated with candy and honey, and then the long and tedious work

24. *Legends of Our Time*, p. 35.
25. The best treatment of the shtetl community is found in the work by Mark Zborowski and Elizabeth Herzog, *Life Is with People* (New York: Schocken Books, 1952). A more poetical, less anthropological account is found in Abraham Joshua Heschel's *The Earth Is the Lord's* (New York: Farrar, Straus, & Giroux, 1950). Also of interest is Lucy Davidowitz's *The Golden Tradition* (Boston: Beacon Press, 1967) and David Roiske's *The Shtetl* (New York: K'tav Publishing House, 1975).

began. The world of his father was the domain of male primacy, the world of religious education. He was forced, almost without warning, to leave a world in which love was automatic and enter a world in which admiration depended upon performance in class.

Wiesel acutely felt this transition from his mother's world of love to the cold, impersonal world of the *Heder,* and although he adjusted well, his yearning to return to the sheltered world of love was quite pronounced. This abrupt shift from one world to another, from infancy to childhood, was psychologically repeated, this time in terrible proportions, in Wiesel's abrupt transition from childhood to adolescence, which was marked by the Nazis' expulsion of the Jews. These two expulsion experiences were in no way equivalent, but in both cases, the transitions were abrupt. Wiesel experienced an inability to return to a previous state of innocence and a rupture of the past which created a void where once there had been fullness. The birth trauma was repeated in the early psychic life of the author in his transition from infancy to childhood, and from childhood to adolescence. There could be no return, and thus the yearning to return increased in intensity.

Conclusions

Throughout this chapter it has been my contention that Wiesel is a heretic, albeit a heretic with profoundly Jewish memories and with a deep love and respect for tradition. Wiesel's thought has evolved from the God-infused world of Eliezer at the beginning of *Night* to the world of *Le Jour* in which God is either indifferent or antagonistic to man. Wiesel's affirmations, when understood in their proper context, are best seen as confessions of the collapse of a meaningful world and as desperate attempts to establish some limited domain of meaning with which to rout the forces of chaos and anomie. Wiesel's affirmations of friendship, community, and love are less exaltations of humanistic values than cries of desperation, attempts to preserve a domain of humanity in a world unconducive to human values. Finally, it has been suggested that there may be some parallel between Wiesel's acute sense of abandonment by God and his sense of abandonment by his mother.

Chapter Four

The Memory of Mystery and the Mystery of Memory

The Mystery of Good

A Beggar in Jerusalem culminates one stage in Wiesel's novels and begins another dimension of exploration. Almost all the characters from the earlier novels are present in this work to witness another aspect of the human mystery, the mystery of good. In addition *A Beggar in Jerusalem* prefigures two of Wiesel's more recent works, *The Oath*, where the madness of a laughing Moshe reappears, and *Ani Maamin*, where the patriarchs again scour the earth and beseech God for their people. David, the narrator of *A Beggar in Jerusalem*, is named after the king of Israel, so hallowed in legend, from whose seed the Messiah was to come. The David in *A Beggar in Jerusalem* experienced a childhood similar to Eliezer's in *Night*. David and Eliezer were born in Transylvania, both were the sons of Sarahs, both were offered the possibility of escape to Palestine but resisted the thought of separation from family, and both experienced the horrors of the Holocaust. Like Michael in *The Town Beyond the Wall* and like the author himself, David returns to the city of his youth. Here he meets the madmen of his childhood, those incarcerated in the local insane asylum. Their madness, like his reality, is marked by the disappearance of the Jewish communities of eastern Europe and the divine implications of their destruction. One incarcerated man comments:

"If truth leads to insanity and if falsehood also leads there, what is left to us? How does God justify Himself in His own eyes, let alone in ours? If the real and the imaginary both culminate in the same scream, in the same laugh, what is creation's purpose, what is its stake? What role is man called upon to play during his mysterious passage on earth?"[1]

Like the correspondent in *Le Jour*, David too knows that "to defeat death, to defeat it by accident, against one's wish, is neither victory nor blessing."[2] As in *Dawn* the setting for the novel is Israel, but in *A Beggar in Jerusalem*, set in 1967, Wiesel depicts a victorious Israel with flashbacks to the anguished moments that preceded victory. Here too, the Israeli characters are portrayed as pragmatic and self-reliant, proud and powerful. One central Israeli character, *Sgan Aluf* (lieutenant colonel) Gad is clearly a redevelopment of Elisha's friend, Gad, in *Dawn*. The Israelis belong to

the new generation which boastfully installed a reign of physical courage and ethical pragmatism. In the eyes of that generation, a people can and must alter its destiny. It believes that the children of Israel can escape the past of Israel. Thus it wishes them all to be healthy, normal, cured of obsessions and complexes, relieved of mystery and burden.[3]

For David and his war companion, Katriel, as for Elisha in *Dawn*, the new generation is deluding itself.[4]

    1. Elie Wiesel, *A Beggar in Jerusalem* (New York: Random House, 1970), p. 28.
    2. *Ibid.*, p. 8.
    3. *Ibid.*, p. 188.
    4. *Ibid.*, p. 188.

As in *The Gates of the Forest*, the narrator falls in love (albeit in a more disguised and far healthier form) with the woman of his former companion-in-arms. Although the love that develops between David and Malka does not really resemble the relationship between Gregor and Clara, the relationship is still triangular. A dead partner is the silent co-participant or witness to the dialogue. Present love is never without the persistent past.

The narration centers around the Western Wall, that sacred vestige of Israel's glorious past and the symbol of hope for the future. The central cast of characters includes the beggars of Jerusalem, each with his own mysteries, his own burden, his own extravagant claims and aspirations. The setting is midnight, the hour when, according to Jewish tradition, the *Shekinah* (the divine presence) would bemoan its exile with the children of Israel. At this hour the pious in Israel would rise to keep the *Shekinah* company in her pain. David, like the author, is really most interested in the internal history of the war and not the external events. The presence of beggars recalls Rebbe Nachman's tale of the seven beggars and the vanished culture of Wiesel's youth. In shtetl culture, beggars occupied a unique place and performed an important role. According to Zborowski and Herzog:

The attitude toward the mendicant is mixed. As an individual who begs, he is despicable. Children who ask for things are told with grown-up disapproval, "Don't be a shnorer!" As an occasion for mitsvos, however, the beggar is an instrument of grace. . . . He presents the extreme example of an interdependence evident in any recipient-donor relationship of the shtetl. Despised and faceless, the beggar nevertheless feels himself at an advantage, because the more fortunate need him as an object of charity. It is he who opens for them the portals of heaven.[5]

5. *Life Is with People*, p. 211.

Wiesel's recollections of the beggar differ significantly from Herzog and Zborowski's descriptions. Wiesel's account is more romantic and imaginative. In a radio address on *A Beggar in Jerusalem,* Wiesel comments:

I like beggars. They belong to the landscape of my youth. Already in *Dawn,* my second book, I described the influences the beggars had on me, that they taught me how to differentiate between night and day. Between silence and language. And between purity and what passes for purity.

The beggars of my childhood are gone, completely gone. They disappeared from the Jewish stage. They vanished nameless, rootless, faceless, tombless. There are no more beggars.[6]

Wiesel's tale provides a haven for the beggars that are no longer (and Wiesel believes that in a sense we are all beggars).[7] Each of the beggars represents a different aspect of the Jewish destiny, a different dimension of the experience of defeat and victory, and a different strategy for the Jewish future in authentic relationship with the Jewish past. I will defer until later a consideration of Wiesel's doctrine of Israel as presented in *A Beggar in Jerusalem.* For the present, I will concentrate on his vision of God and the human encounter.

Anshel, the beggar who played with children, embodies the Jewish sense of compassion. Troubled by victory as he once was by defeat, Anshel sees the scars of defeat in the faces of Arab youngsters.

Victor, he? A borrowed role, a borrowed life. He blushes each time a Mohammed, a Jamil pulls at his sleeve. Theirs are not borrowed roles. Victors may not all resemble one another but

---

6. Elie Wiesel, "Jerusalem, the Symbol of Survival," A Radio Address, N.B.C. Radio Network, June 14, 1970 under the Eternal Light Series of the Jewish Theological Seminary.
    7. *Ibid.*

the vanquished do. The vanquished everywhere wear the same dark haunted look, the same pleading smile. Vanquished children are everywhere the same. In a world in ruins, selling ruins is all they have left.[8]

Confronted by the human consequences of the Israeli victory in the Six Day War, the human consequences of a defeated Arab population, the narrator comments on Anshel's reaction. "All the same, for the victor that he is, victory is gradually losing not its significance, not its necessity, but its taste of joy."[9]

Zaddok, whose name means the righteous one, represents the dimension of prayer. This beggar claims that his prayers earned Israel her victory. Another beggar, Moshe the madman, comments ironically, "To hell with you and your prayers. Beware of anyone praying in times of war, that's what my father taught his children."[10] The irony of Moshe's comment is not really apparent unless the reader is familiar with Rabbinic legend. One of the most well known of the Rabbinic legends dealing with a military crisis in Israel's history describes Moses in a turmoil as Israel approaches the Sea.[11] Surrounded by enemies on one side and the sea on the other, Moshe *Rabbenu* (Moses our teacher) beseeches God in prayer. God rebukes Moses saying, "there is a time for prayer and a time for action." According to Rabbi Elazar, God could never have

8. *A Beggar in Jerusalem*, p. 17.
9. *Ibid.* John W. Dixon, Jr.'s critical review of Weisel's expression of the Jewish attitude toward the 1967 victory fails to notice the compassion of Anshel. Dixon proves insensitive to the "necessity" of the victory for the Jewish people and to their refusal to accept a defeated status. See John W. Dixon, Jr. "Voice of Ecstasy" in the *Christian Century* (June 17, 1970), pp. 761–762.
10. *A Beggar in Jerusalem*, p. 10.
11. See *Babalonia Talmud Sotah* 36,37. *Midrash Shemot Rabbah* 21, *Mechilta Beshalach Va Yehi* 5.

made so heretical a statement. He must have said, "There is a time for long prayer and a time for short prayer."[12] Similarly, Wiesel's Moshe (*Moshe* is the Hebrew for Moses) has learned his lesson well. When Israel was in trouble, Wiesel's Moshe sang. Again, in a moment of crisis, he anticipated the joy of victory and responded, as his earlier namesake had responded in the triumphant song of the sea. This time, however, the Israelis themselves had to create an occasion for the song. Here too, as in the Rabbinic legends of the sea, it was only when the Israelis had jumped into the water up to their necks that the sea began to part.[13] Nonetheless, God is no longer the active agent. As Robert Alter comments on Wiesel's work: "the theological center has shifted to the human spirit; it is pathetically finite man who is the source of miraculous aspiration, of regeneration in a world where all life is inevitably transient."[14] Another of the beggars is named Dan, which in Hebrew means Judge. Dan embodies the cosmopolitan wisdom of the Jewish people. A prince among men, the master of many disguises, Dan also embodies the option of madness, a moral prophetic madness.[15]

Man has become dehumanized, horror is piled on horror, evil on evil. Fraternity, solidarity: words, words that don't even make one laugh anymore. Show me a single group achieving human dignity and I'll hurry back to join it; show me a single peaceful corner and I'll gladly return to settle there. But there is no such thing and you know it. Your entire universe is crumbling with

12. *Midrash Shemot Rabbah* 21.
13. *Midrash Shemot Rabbah* 81.
14. Robert Alter, *After the Tradition: Essays on Modern Jewish Writing* (New York: E. P. Putnam & Co., Inc., 1971), p. 160.
15. For an excellent discussion of madness in the works of Elie Wiesel, see Byron Sherwin, "Elie Wiesel on Madness" in *Journal, Central Conference American Rabbis* (June 1972), pp. 24–32.

violence and hatred. Old against young, white against black, poor against rich. Yesterday's holocaust will be followed by tomorrow's, and *that* one will be total![16]

There are other beggars. Shlomo the blind man sees clearly and personifies the spirit of waiting (for the Messiah) that so marked the pre-Holocaust Jew. "He must come. When? I don't know. Who am I to know? He knows, that's enough for me."[17] Velvel is the beggar who laughs and Ezra (Ezra is Hebrew for help), the son of Abraham, is the beggar who cries.

One of the tales told by David in *A Beggar in Jerusalem* most clearly illustrates an important aspect of much of Holocaust literature in general and Wiesel's own work in particular. Holocaust literature (tales and stories as opposed to more abstract thought, such as history, theology, or psychology) restores personality to the victims and casts aside the anonymity that most characterized death during the Holocaust. No scene in the art of the Holocaust has captured the horror of anonymous death more vividly for me than the execution scene in *Seven Beauties*. The major character and his companion were sitting under a tree when far in the distance they saw the execution of a number of Jews, an execution that failed to interrupt the lunch of the commanding officer. The long angle of the camera's vision accentuated the impersonal quality of the detached and momentary killing that had no lasting consequences for the executioner. The victims do not protest; there are no final farewells, no acts of heroism, not even a moment's hesitation. The deed is done in the distance. The task is completed, and the officer finishes his lunch. Contrast this scene with an execution

16. *A Beggar in Jerusalem*, p. 42.
17. *Ibid.*, p. 9.

scene narrated by David in *A Beggar in Jerusalem*. First
the Rebbe exhorts his disciples to bravery and "the blasphemy" of faith. Then the President and the notables are
executed. Next Tevye, the tailor, arranges his family in
one final gesture of solidarity and protest in the name of
civility. The master and his disciples then line up. The
killers are wearied by their action. A disciple begins to
sing, and the Rebbe joins him. The soldiers shoot, and the
man continues to sing. The Nazi officer confronts the
singing disciple who refuses to die and makes him aware of
his status as the lone survivor. "Shaking from head to toe,
breathless, he [the officer] looks at the disciple and falls to
his knees and speaks to him the way one speaks to a
conqueror, a victor shrouded in mystery."[18]

Which way did death occur during the Holocaust? Undoubtedly, both ways, but in mass murder of such magnitude the impersonal was predominant. In Wiesel's work,
as in much of Holocaust literature, death is restored to its
human place as an event in the life of real people. It ceases
to be anonymous. The literature is therapeutic, at points
even restorative, even if it less than accurately charac-
terizes the events as they occurred and thus runs the risk
of falsification and mystification.

At their meeting in front of the Wall, each of the
beggars tells his tale, each claims credit for his victory,
and each seeks to understand the nature of that victory
and its deeper meaning. Wiesel conveys certain cosmic
associations with the meeting at the Wall. David, the king
whose name, in legend, is associated with the Messianic
hope, is joined by Malka (Hebrew for Queen), the name
for the feminine manifestation of God according to Jewish
mystical tradition. Malka is the wife of Katriel, David's

18. *Ibid.*, p. 80.

comrade during the war who lost his life after the return to the Western Wall. Katriel's name is also significant since Katriel means the crown of God. The root word *Keter* (Hebrew for crown) is the name associated with the highest manifestation of God in the Jewish mystical tradition. The tales that are told during the evening occasion the construction of two powerful mythic understandings of the reasons for Israel's victory. According to these tales, Israel won the war because the Jews were united as one and because the Jewish people could deploy six million more names in battle.[19] I shall return to consider the sociological implications of these conclusions later. For the present I would like to examine the spiritual and ontological dimensions of Wiesel's treatment of the Six Day War.

Several critics have commented that Wiesel argues in *A Beggar in Jerusalem* that although the Torah given at Sinai was taken back at Auschwitz, it was returned to Israel in Jerusalem. A. Roy Eckardt uses this reading of *A Beggar in Jerusalem* as the basis of his own meditation on the meaning of the covenant in contemporary theology.[20] Byron Sherwin argues in a similar vein in his impressive paper "Wiesel's Midrash: The Writings of Elie Wiesel and Their Relationship to Jewish Tradition."[21] Sherwin writes:

Does God's breaking the covenant mean that the covenant is broken, disregarded at the end? While Wiesel raises this question, his final position is that the covenant, while broken by God, has not been terminated. Echoing Jacob Gladstein's poetic statement that God gave the Torah at Sinai and took it back at

19. *Ibid.*, p. 202. See also chapter 6 of this work.
20. A. Roy Eckardt, "The Covenant After the Holocaust," to be published in Irving Greenberg and Alvin Rosenfeld, eds., *Confronting the Holocaust* (Bloomington: Indiana University Press, forthcoming).
21. Sherwin's work is also scheduled for publication in the Greenberg and Rosenfeld volume.

Auschwitz, Wiesel adds that *God returned the Torah* to Israel at
the Western Wall.[22] (italics mine)

The passage that Sherwin cites as his proof text occurs
toward the end of *A Beggar in Jerusalem* and forms the
nucleus of David's conclusions about the presence or absence of God during the Six Day War. David remarks that
the Jews' return to Jerusalem in 1967 marked the third
time in which all of Israel marched together from the four
corners of the universe. The first time was at Sinai, the
second at Auschwitz, and the third was in Jerusalem.
(Elsewhere, Wiesel adds a forth moment on Simchat
Torah in Moscow). David comments:

> Just like long ago, at Sinai, when they were given the Torah.
> Just like a generation ago, in the kingdom of night, when it was
> taken back. Once again the exiles are being gathered in, the knot
> is being knotted — the end is rejoining the beginning and justify-
> ing it. Over there, in the camp, a wise and pious inmate had
> cried out in a fit of madness: "All of us heard God in the desert;
> here we shall be allowed to see Him." — "Yes," the others had
> answered, "we shall see Him and perish." The image of God
> cannot be transmitted; it can be carried away only in death.
> Here, it is man's image that is being transmitted. And in order to
> receive it, an entire people had begun to march for the third time
> in its history.[23]

I think that once again Sherwin is mistaken in his reading
of Wiesel. The people have come together in Jerusalem
not to hear the word of God nor to witness the anti-
revelation of the anti-God in the kingdom of Night. It is not
God whose image is being transmitted or whose presence
is made known. Rather, the people come together to confront the presence of the Jewish past, a past whose pres-

22. Sherwin, p. 12.
23. *A Beggar in Jerusalem*, p. 200.

ence thus contains the memory of God. Now, however, the image of God has been replaced by the image of man, the image of a people who have routed defeat and survived, in community, in celebration, and in relationship with a past that is being transmitted. The void has been bridged, in solidarity, in hope, in despair, in pain, and in violence. Theologically, as Robert Alter has correctly pointed out, the center has shifted to the human spirit.

Furthermore, it must also be emphasized that the novel does not conclude with the revelation of human potential and the reappropriation of the Jewish past. Rather, as at Sinai where the revelation of God was followed by the construction of a Golden Calf, the moment of celebration and triumph wanes, the long night's assembly at the Wall gives way to the crowds of the day. The storyteller is left to ponder the question of *Dawn:* what does it mean to kill another, to take another's life? What does the change of roles mean, the movement from vanquished to victor?

A victor, he? Victory does not prevent suffering from having existed, nor death from having taken its toll. How can one work for the living without by that very act betraying those who are absent? The question remains open, and no new fact can change it. Of course, the mystery of good is no less disturbing than the mystery of evil. But one does not cancel out the other. Man alone is capable of uniting them by remembering.[24]

The consciousness of the Jewish people is now further complicated. The people must unite the memory of God and the anti-God, Sinai and Auschwitz. Both memories must be united with Jerusalem and that brief, glowing moment of hope and triumph. But even Jerusalem of 1967 gives way at the end of the book to "Christiansted" of

24. *A Beggar in Jerusalem,* p. 210.

1968. We dare not yearn for the enduring moment, yet we cannot forget the moment we hoped would endure.

The Mystery of Memory

IN *Souls on Fire* Wiesel assumes the position of a teacher of the tradition, thus augmenting his earlier stances as a teacher of his people and a teller of tales. In *Souls on Fire* the tales Wiesel tells are at first glance less his own. Only at the end of the work does the narrator interject his personal perspective, suggesting that the stories are his versions of the tradition rather than objective representations. Hoping to avoid the controversy that surrounded Martin Buber's representation of Hasidic tales,[25] Wiesel writes:

> . . . now it is my turn to show them the way I saw them as a child, as I see them still. They are subjective, incomplete, these portraits, with their share of unavoidable repetitions, errors and gaps. They may well say more about the narrator than about his characters.[26]

The goal of the story teller is "to tell of himself while telling of others. He wishes . . . but to close gaps and create new bonds."[27] Wiesel has nonetheless succeeded in conveying a sense of the Hasidic spirit, perhaps not with scholarly detachment but with the gaze of fervor. Wiesel is the filter and not the scholar. He is in the center; the child he was is in dialogue with both the Holocaust and the post-Holocaust world. Hence his treatment of Hasidism is

---

25. See Gershom Scholem, "Martin Buber's Interpretation of Hasidism," in *The Messianic Idea in Judaism* (New York: Schocken Books, 1971), pp. 227–251, and Martin Buber's rejoinder "Interpreting Hasidism," in *Commentary,* Vol. 36, No. 3 (September 1963).

26. *Souls on Fire,* p. 258.

27. *Ibid.,* p. 259.

all the more instructive for any understanding of Wiesel as a religious thinker.

The choice of titles for this work is also significant. The work first appeared in French, and the French title, *Célébration Hasidique* (Hasidic Celebration), obviously differs from the English title *Souls on Fire*, which might have been designed for the American audience's association with Eldridge Cleaver's *Soul on Ice*. The double association of fire with the fires of passion and fervor, and the fires of the ovens of Auschwitz also provides greater depth and mystery to the title, greater contrast, greater associative value. Students of Holocaust literature might also recall Jakov Lind's collection of short stories (published eight years earlier), which describes the frantic, fantastic madness of the Holocaust and post-Holocaust periods entitled *Soul of Wood*. An interesting juxtaposition is struck between the Black man's soul on ice, frozen by persecution, the world's soul of wood, hard and unfeeling, and the Jewish soul on fire, burning and consumed. Wiesel can never forget the fires of Auschwitz, and he shares this inability to forget with his readers.

Several themes dominate the tales Wiesel tells, themes that were prevalent in Hasidism and have likewise been prevalent in the corpus of Wiesel's literature. Whenever Wiesel approaches the legends from the outside and assumes the perspective of observer, the community's need predominates, while when he enters into the inner dynamics of the legendary material itself and speaks in his own voice, the quality of hope, yearning, and triumph dominates. Wiesel then attempts to relate the tales to contemporary life, and in this effort he assumes the role of moral teacher or even preacher.

28. *The Gates of the Forest*, p. 199.

In *The Gates of the Forest* Gregor-Gavriel made peace with the Hasidic world of his youth as he made peace with his own weakness and limitations. He and the Rebbe struggled not as master and disciple but as equals; both triumphed and both were defeated. Gregor's defeat came when the Rebbe asked him, "What is there left for us to do?"[28] Here too Wiesel realizes the validity of the Rebbe's question and points toward the human needs to which Hasidism responded. Wiesel here is not merely the outsider or the scholar who can speak of the neutralization of messianism in early Hasidism, where the messianic yearnings for redemption were replaced by the ecstatic communal celebrations and the individual strivings for salvation. Rather, his tone is one of involvement and engagement even though his perspective is that of the outsider. Wiesel speaks of the needs of the community.

They needed to believe that God took an interest in His creation, that He listened to all the voices; they needed to believe that miracles were still possible, even for them.[29]

For the Hasidic community, the pain of exile was eased if not momentarily replaced by the ecstasy of celebration. Although a mass movement that opened the gates of mysticism to the unlettered multitude, Hasidism still placed a major emphasis on the individual. Wiesel sees the Hasidic emphasis on the individual soul and its quest for salvation as a rebellion against the powerlessness and meaninglessness of the isolated individual. This need for power was the second need toward which Hasidism responded:

The individual is not a cog in a monstrous machine; it is within his power to modify the very laws which imprison him and the

29. *Souls on Fire*, p. 35.

very relationship maintained by the Judge with the accused and witnesses.[30]

The post-Holocaust consciousness only intensifies Wiesel's perception of the needs of East European Jewry. Wiesel writes of the Magid of Mezeritch and his desire to train spiritual leaders:

. . . perhaps he intuitively knew that European Jewry was embarking on a long and bloody journey, and that it would need all the help and support it could get.[31]

Not only does the consciousness of the Holocaust intensify Wiesel's depiction of the needs of East European Jewry, it also painfully undercuts their accomplishments. Although they needed to believe that miracles were possible, "Death negates miracles, the death of one million children negates more than miracles."[32]

Eliezer's journey into the kingdom of *Night* is portrayed by Wiesel as the dialectic negation of the journey of the Baal Shem, the founder of Hasidism. The Baal Shem's tales try to "prove that man is more than he appears to be and that he is capable of giving more than he appears to possess."[33] The Baal Shem was "Obsessed by eternity, he neglected history and let himself be carried by legend."[34] Eliezer was literally carried off by history, a tragic history that trampled over legends. Wiesel's tales do not allow us to forget that man is less than he imagines himself to be. Obsessed by eternity, Eliezer learned the frightening lessons of history that Wiesel transformed into contemporary legend.

30. *Ibid.*, p. 33.
31. *Ibid.*, p. 77.
32. *Ibid.*, p. 37.
33. *Ibid.*, p. 7.
34. *Ibid.*, p. 8.

In *Dawn* Elisha learned that waiting for the Messiah
may not suffice; the pressing problems of history force the
Jew to act. In *The Gates of the Forest* Wiesel narrated the
tale of Joseph di-la Reina, a famous medieval Cabalist,
who decided to force God's hand and to bring the Messiah
only to be deceived by his own compassion. "The poor
miracle-maker," Wiesel writes, "had a heart which wasn't
hard enough."[35] Similarly, *Souls on Fire* is filled with tales
in which the Zaddik, the righteous master, almost suc-
ceeds in putting an end to history. Perhaps the radicalness
of *Dawn* and of *A Beggar in Jerusalem* cannot be fully
understood unless we appreciate the complexity of this
legendary tradition. Rabbinic, Mystical, and Hasidic
Judaism all firmly believed that Jewish piety was the messianic, redemptive strategy of the Jewish people.
Whenever the Jews were hurt by a messianic movement,
the following generations emphasized the divine role in
bringing the messiah (while stressing in only a minor way
the human responsibility so as to maintain the redemptive
meaning of individual piety). In Hasidism, a movement
that developed in the wake of and partially in response to
Sabbateanism (the messianic movement of the late seven-
teenth century which had an enormous yet suppressed
influence on Judaism)[36] the tension between messianism
and responsibility is acute. Consequently, in the Hasidic
tradition of the following generations there are many
legends in which the messianic arrival is imminent and yet

35. *The Gates of the Forest*, p. 18.
36. Gershom Scholem, *Sabbatai Sevi: The Mystical Messiah*,
translated by R. J. Zwi Werblowsky (Princeton: Princeton University
Press, 1973). Also Gershom Scholem, *Major Trends in Jewish Mysti-
cism* (New York: Schocken Books, 1946), pp. 287–300; Scholem, *The
Messianic Idea in Judaism*, pp. 176–203; and Rivka Shatz-Oppeheimer,
*Hasidism As Mysticism (Quietistic Elements in 18th Century Hasidic
Thought)* (Jerusalem: Magnes Press, 1968).

for all sorts of reasons it must be deferred.[37] Wiesel's retelling of these tales emphasizes both the individual act of piety as one step in the redemptive drama and the despair that resulted from the period of delay. Wiesel underscores both the sense of hope and the sense of disappointment. The Hasidim, as Wiesel described them, lived on the edge, always waiting, always hoping that perhaps this time the end would come. Wiesel is gentle in his treatment of this Hasidic posture of waiting; he allows the reader to share the sense of excitement and anticipation as well as the sense of disappointment. Elisha in *Dawn* had to deal with the reality of disappointment (as do most of Wiesel's characters throughout his other works), but in *Souls on Fire* the gentle hope predominates. Wiesel depicts this messianic tradition of imminent arrival as a triumph of the human spirit, a triumph of hope in a world of despair. He writes:

If the Baal Shem could have met Rabbi Haim Ben-Atar . . . the two men would have hastened the coming of the Messiah, or so says Hasidic tradition, *with the stress on the encounter.* Every encounter quickens the steps of the Redeemer; let two human beings become one and the world is no longer the same; let two human creatures accept one another and creation will have meaning, the meaning they will have imposed upon it.[38] (italics mine)

The narrator stresses the encounter and the isolated responsibility of the individual rather than the deeds of all humanity. Hasidism assumed that the cosmos is in basic, if muffled, harmony with human (Jewish) aspiration.

The emphasis on human responsibility for creating

37. See Gershom Scholem, "The Neutralization of the Messianic Element in Early Hasidism" in *The Messianic Idea in Judaism,* pp. 176–203.

meaning and for imposing it upon the universe and God is unique in Wiesel's treatment of Hasidism. This emphasis comes to the fore in *Souls on Fire* as a new means of understanding and confronting God. I stress that the emphasis on man is unique to Wiesel; this perspective is present in Hasidic tradition, though not dominant. In Wiesel's treatment of Hasidism the theological center has shifted fully to the human spirit, and here the human spirit is not miserable or finite, as in *A Beggar in Jerusalem,* but rather aspiring, uplifted, longing for the divine.

The key to this new emphasis may have been provided by a biographical incident that is noted by Harry Cargas in his recent work *Harry James Cargas in Conversation with Elie Wiesel.* In Cargas's work Elie Wiesel recalls a visit he and his mother once made to a rebbe. In that visit the rebbe told his mother:

Sarah, daughter of David . . . I want you to know that one day your son will grow up to be a great man in Israel but neither you nor I will be alive to see it.[39]

Wiesel later used this same scene of his mother's visit to the rebbe in *A Beggar in Jerusalem* where Sarah, now the mother of David rather than the daughter of David, goes to the rebbe and hears the identical blessing/curse. Prior to her visit, Sarah prayed a mother's prayer for her son:

"Let my son fear God and love man; that's what I wish for him. Let him love God but only through man: that would satisfy me. What I don't want, Rebbe, is that he fear God through man."[40]

In *Souls on Fire* the emphasis on man is complete. Wiesel first bespeaks this emphasis in the name of the Baal

38. *Souls on Fire,* p. 33.
39. *Harry James Cargas in Conversation with Elie Wiesel,* p. 75.
40. *A Beggar in Jerusalem,* p. 68.

Shem's followers. It should be noted that Wiesel does not speak in their voice or use their beliefs in his own name. Rather, he describes and analyzes the Baal Shem's followers; the distance between them and Wiesel is not erased. All post-Holocaust consciousness of God is dialectical. The pre-Holocaust consciousness was different. The Baal Shem's followers lived in a world in which the divine presence and the assurance of meaning were unchallenged. Wiesel writes:

For the Baal Shem's followers, God is not neutral. Nor is He an abstraction. He is at once ally and judge of man inside creation. The bond between them is irreplaceable, it is love. God himself needs love. Whoever loves God will be loved in turn, loved by man and loved by God. It is in man that God must be loved, because the love of God goes through the love of man. Whoever loves God exclusively, namely, excluding man, reduces his love and his God to the level of abstraction. Beshtian Hasidism denies all abstraction.[41]

Elsewhere, when Wiesel is no longer speaking in the name of the followers, his emphasis on the role of man becomes more extreme. Commenting on the verse "know what is higher than you," Wiesel writes that all events originate with man. It is only through man that God manifests himself.

The fascination with the individual's power to resist God, which was developed in Wiesel's early works, is continued in *Souls on Fire*. Wiesel loves the human spirit that resists God and sees it as most necessary in the contemporary situation. Speaking of the Kotzker Rebbe, Wiesel writes:

Thus it is not really surprising that Mendl of Kotzk should have praised the unsuspected qualities of a Pharaoh; he knew, that

41. *Souls on Fire*, p. 31.

one, how to defy God! "What a fellow," the Rebbe marveled,
"he didn't cringe as soon as the blows started falling; he perse-
vered!" What is important is to accept the challenge, to fight the
battle; what is important is to choose an opponent more powerful than oneself."[42]

Pedro's discussion with Michael echoes in this' passage.
Similarly, in his portrayal of Rebbe Nachman of Bratzlav
(the greatest of the Hasidic storytellers), Wiesel is fascinated by Nachman's ability to resist God and to struggle
with God.

To blindly submit to God, without questioning the meaning of
this submission, would be to diminish Him. To want to understand Him would be to reduce His intentions, His vision to the
level of ours. How then can man take himself seriously? Revolt
is not a solution, neither is submission. Remains laughter,
metaphysical laughter.[43]

Modern man must discover the strength to laugh, to
create, to meet the challenges of the human situation.
Wiesel sees the contemporary task as similar to the
Hasidic task. We must fight sadness with joy. "One must
impose meaning on what perhaps has none and draw
ecstasy from nameless faceless pain."[44] Our task is to fight
solitude and thus to fight death. Above all, Wiesel sees the
contemporary need to affirm life. The Torah commands
vehai ahem (you shall live by them [by these statutes]).
According to the Hasidism that Wiesel teaches,

Torah is given to man so he may celebrate life and everything
that makes life a source of celebration.[45]

Despite the optimism of Wiesel's tales and of his recol-

42. *Ibid.*, p. 236.
43. *Ibid.*, pp. 198–199.
44. *Ibid.*, pp. 35–36.
45. *Ibid.*, p. 60.

lections of Hasidism, Wiesel continually reminds the readers of the great abyss that separates our world from the world of his childhood. He writes of the transformation in his understanding of Rebbe Levi Yitchak of Berdichiv, the great defender of the Jewish people:

Protector of Israel, he pleaded for any and all Jews unjustly accused and unjustly punished. His most beautiful adventures, the most beautiful accounts and stories of his adventures, are those that show him in his role of attorney for the defense, challenging and remonstrating the Judge. As a child, I loved them and saw in them nothing but love and friendship. Today I feel their weight of despair and revolt — and love them even more. I often look at them; I owe them much. Sometimes I dip my pen into their wealth before I write.[46]

Similarly, in *The Gates of the Forest* Wiesel recounts the story in which the Baal Shem would go to a forest, light a fire, and say a prayer when evil was about to befall the Jewish people. When similar problems arose in the next generation, the Baal Shem's disciple knew where to find the spot in the forest and how to light the fire. Even though he had forgotten the prayer, evil was averted. In the next generation, the fire was forgotten but the spot was recalled, and this, too, was sufficient. Finally, in the next generation, the spot, the fire, and the prayer were forgotten. All that remained was the tale. In *The Gates of the Forest* Wiesel concludes this tale by remarking that God created man because he loves stories, while in *Souls on Fire* Wiesel reminds us that the telling of the tale is no longer sufficient. *"The proof is that the threat has not been averted."*[47] Elsewhere, in *Souls on Fire,* Wiesel reminds us that it is not sufficient to call the Messiah to

46. *Ibid.,* p. 91.
47. *Ibid.,* p. 168.

make him come. Wiesel's earlier lyricism has become more biting, more bitter. We of the post-Holocaust period must reaffirm life, but not with the grandiose hope of redemption that was the root of Hasidic affirmations. The sparks that we redeem are isolated. We must nonetheless muster our power, Wiesel tells us, in order to prevent an easy victory for death. Death should not win cheaply, for in the world of the void there is no hope beyond life.

Chapter Five

A Change of Perspective

FOUR OF Wiesel's latest works exhibit a marked change in his sociological perspective without any real shift in his theological vision. In *The Oath, Ani Maamin,* and *Zalman or The Madness of God,* Wiesel does not deny his vision of the void. On the contrary, he continually confirms the truth of his bleak vision although he does challenge the personal and sociological value of facing such a truth. In these works Wiesel begins to fear the consequence of his vision, the justification of his witness. In *Messengers of God,* Wiesel once again assumes the stance of an interpreter of Jewish tradition. This time he is burdened by his role of leadership within the Jewish community, and this burden of leadership imposes itself on the Midrashic material he interprets.

The Oath: The Role of Witness and the Desperate Appeal toward Life

Wiesel's novel *The Oath* is the tale of an old man's desperate attempt to convince a young man of the futility of his contemplated suicide. The old man is the last survivor of the village of his youth, Kolvillag. Kolvillag is the combination of the Hebrew *kol,* which means every, and the Hungarian *villag,* which means village; and Kolvillag represents the prototypical *shtetl* whose destruction at the hands of a mad enemy is seen by the narrator as a precursor of the Holocaust.[1] The old man of *The Oath* had been entrusted with the tale of Kolvillag, the chronicle of its entire history, yet he was commanded to silence by the village saint and threatened with *herem,* excommunication, if he revealed the tale. The young man is also a survivor, yet he is without a tale. He is the child of concentration camp victims who are living in a past they cannot convey to their child. When the mother looks at her son, she cannot even see him and sees only their former son killed in the camps. The young man can be brought back from the brink of the abyss only by the tale that the old man tells.

Two major shifts in Wiesel's position are expressed in *The Oath.* The first shift involves a re-examination of the role of witness. Wiesel questions the relative value of silence and words. He finally narrows his expectations concerning the impact of witness from the cosmic or historical dimension to the personal dimension. The second shift involves a positive affirmation of life which moves beyond despair. Wiesel has moved from a protest against death to an outright appeal to life. Both shifts strongly coalesce around Moshe the madman, a character present in many of Wiesel's novels and short stories[2] and a central character in *The Oath.* In *The Oath* Moshe is a brave saint

1. After the destruction of Kolvillag, the old man comments: "And suddenly I understood with every fiber of my being why I was shuddering at this vision of horror. *I had just glimpsed the future.*" (Elie Wiesel, *The Oath,* p. 281; italics mine.)

2. See *Night,* "Moshe the Madman," in *Legends of Our Time, The Town Beyond the Wall,* and *A Beggar in Jerusalem.*

who pleads guilty to a murder he did not commit in order to prevent the destruction of Kolvillag. Moshe soon discovers, however, that his sacrifice was futile and that the Jewish population would still be blamed and consequently destroyed. In the wake of the destruction, Moshe addresses the Jewish community and demands of them a vow of silence and the extinction of the Jewish memory.

"This Jewish memory not only robbed the executioner of his final victory, it haunted and punished him by reminding him of his crimes and citing them as examples and warnings for the benefit of mankind present and future.

. . . Yet the more they hate us, the more we shout our love of man; the more they mock us, the more we shout our attachment to history. The enemy can do with us as he pleases, but never will he silence us — that has been our motto.

. . . Put an end to it once and for all. We have been mankind's memory and heart too long. Too long have we been other nations' laughingstock. Our stories have either amused or annoyed them. Now we shall adopt a new way: silence.

. . . We are going to impose the ultimate challenge, not by language but by absence of language, not by the word but by the abdication of the word."[3]

For the narrator Moshe's words suggested a new path, for if suffering and memory are intrinsically linked, then perhaps the former can be destroyed by attacking the latter. The narrator recalls: "But I saw in Moshe's mysterious protest a paradox — it incited to joy, to fulfillment through joy, rather than to despair."[4]

Wiesel's difficulties with the role of witness are not entirely new. In *One Generation After* he was also frus-

3. *The Oath*, pp. 237–239.
4. *Ibid.*, p. 240.

trated by the futility of the role. The world's relationship to the Jews and the persistent persecution of other peoples caused Wiesel to question the efficacy of witness and the ultimate faith in man that such a witness implies.[5] Wiesel argued that little has been learned if society has changed so little. He also expressed his fear that words might betray the dead, for words threaten the mystery behind experience as well as the intensity and the immediacy of experience itself. Although Wiesel was frustrated by the struggle to articulate the ineffable, he persisted in his endeavor, and *One Generation After* was another attempt to bear witness to the Holocaust. In *The Oath* Wiesel attempts to resolve the tension between the need to bear witness and the desire to remain silent.

In *The Oath* the witness obeys Moshe's command to remain silent until he is faced with the opportunity of saving one human life. The witness has narrowed his perspective; he no longer expects to save the world or to bring the awaited redemption but rather to challenge a single man and his relationship with other men. Rather than performing a cosmic, ontic, or even historical function, the witness's task is now limited to the individual. The witness is able to teach a man how to proceed beyond despair without affirming the beauty or meaning of life. The secret that the witness can convey most forcefully is the futility of death. Rather than argue, as does Emil Fackenheim, that the Jew is forbidden to despair of man lest he cooperate in giving the world over to the forces of Auschwitz,[6] Wiesel argues that despair is justified but that death is no solution. The old man said to his young companion, "I am not telling you not to despair of man, I only

5. "One Generation After," in *One Generation After*, pp. 8–17.
6. See the discussion of Emil Fackenheim in chapter 7 of this work.

ask you not to offer death one more victim, one more
victory. It does not deserve it, believe me.''[7]

This narrowing of the task of witness is consistent with
the humanism that Wiesel develops in *The Oath*. In a real
sense this humanism is an extension of the limited human
focus that the Spaniard, Pedro, embodied in *The Town
Beyond the Wall*, but now in *The Oath* it is clothed in a
Jewish fabric. Unlike the Spaniard, the old man of *The
Oath* was raised in the *shtetl* and nurtured on the mysteries of Judaism. The old man speaks in a Jewish idiom
and uses Jewish symbols.

The true contest must take place on the level of the individual. It
is here, in the present, that the Temple is reclaimed or de-
molished. . . . The mystery of the universe resides not in the
universe but in man; perfection can be attained only by the
individual.[8]

The old man argues that to defeat evil one must begin by
helping one's brother.

The concept of the Messiah in *The Oath* is similarly
narrowed to human dimensions. The old man rejects the
grand vision of the Messiah. He remembers the teaching of
Moshe the madman and the example of his life; ''What is
the Messiah, you [Moshe] said, if not man transcending his
solitude in order to make his fellow-man less solitary?''[9]
At another point the old man describes Moshe:

He could gamble with his own suffering, but not with that of
someone for whom suffering was not a game. He knew that
nothing justifies the pain man causes another. Any messiah in
whose name men are tortured can only be a false messiah. It is
by diminishing evil, present and real evil, experienced evil, that

7. *The Oath*, p. 12.
8. *Ibid.*, p. 14.
9. *Ibid.*, p. 80.

one builds the city of the sun. It is by helping the person who looks at you with tears in his eyes, needing help, needing you or at least your presence, that you may attain perfection.[10]

There may be no single Messiah, but there are many messianic moments when the barrier of solitude is penetrated and the burden of suffering is lessened.

A well-known Hasidic tale may serve as a model for the limited perspective that Wiesel presents in *The Oath* as it did for his conclusion in *The Gates of the Forest*. The story is told of a Rebbe grown old who once confessed that in his youth he wanted to bring the Messiah, as he matured he wanted to improve the world, as he grew older he wanted to influence his community, at the end of his life he sought to change his family, and finally, in his old age, he came to see that the real struggle was to change himself. The young Wiesel sought to force God's hand; the writer of *The Oath* is content to influence a single soul. It is critical to note that the individual act is not offered as the smaller part of a greater drama as are the commandments in Lurrianic Kabbalism. According to Lurrianic Kabbalism, each fulfillment of God's commandment reunites the sparks scattered by the cosmic catastrophe of creation. Each mitzvah performs an ontic function.[11] There is no such grandiosity to Wiesel's vision. On the contrary, the humanism that is presented in *The Oath* does not represent a cosmic dimension. Thus, the witness violates an oath to save *one* human life.

Although Wiesel does resolve the problem of witness insofar as it can be justified to save a human life, he does not fully resolve the theme of silence which he develops in

10. *Ibid.*, p. 138.
11. See Gershon Scholem, *Major Trends in Jewish Mysticism*, pp. 244–286, and the discussion of Lurrianic Mysticism in chapter 6 of this work.

conjunction with the theme of witness. In *The Oath* Wiesel continues to flirt with the mystical and romantic notion of silence that he expressed in *One Generation After*. In *One Generation After* Wiesel imagined that the vision of the Holocaust might have been transmitted more effectively by a mystical withdrawal from words. Speaking of the survivors he said:

Had all of them remained mute, their accumulated silences would have become unbearable: the impact would have deafened the world.[12]

Clearly, Wiesel's expectations from silence were enormous. It is difficult to imagine that people who had proven themselves indifferent to words would have been sensitive to the voices of silence. In *The Oath* Moshe also expected much from the silence he imposed on the community of Kolvillag. For Moshe silence is "an unexplored path, one which does not lead to the outside, to expression."[13] Silence is the instrument by which the Jew can break the circle of suffering which leads from persecution to witness, from witness to persecution. Moshe is optimistic. In his speech, he proclaims:

"We shall do it without the help of the Messiah; he is taking too long. We shall start right here. I have found the method . . ."[14]

Silence is that method.

Despite Moshe's optimism, Wiesel fails to present either a clear or convincing argument to substantiate the efficacy of silence. A number of possible lines of argument can be derived from the work, but Wiesel does not sufficiently develop any of them in a complete or persua-

12. *One Generation After*, p. 13.
13. *The Oath*, p. 239.
14. *Ibid.*

sive manner. The different arguments do not coalesce, and the theme of silence thus remains disjointed.

One broad argument for the efficacy of silence is presented in *The Oath* by the old man.

If suffering and the history of suffering were intrinsically united, then the one could be abolished by attacking the other; by ceasing to refer to the events of the present, we would forestall ordeals in the future.[15]

However, the intrinsic link between suffering and the history of suffering is not explained or developed. Will silence merely forestall ordeals in the future as the old man seems to suggest,[16] or will it eliminate the problem of Jewish suffering as Moshe seems to promise?[17] Will silence end the cycle of persecution by reducing the persecutor's guilt and hence his need to silence his accusers, or will silence merely confine suffering to the present by not perpetuating it through memory? Will silence end the Jew's role as the conscience of humanity (Wiesel's reading of "a light unto nations") and hence the world's need to destroy that conscience, or will it reduce suffering because the telling of the tale creates an appetite for death in the perverse minds of potential murderers?

Wiesel's position is difficult since any of these alternatives places him perilously close to positions he has strenuously rejected. For example, if Wiesel were to maintain that silence will terminate the Jews' role as the conscience of mankind, he would be in basic sympathy with Sigmund Freud's radical suggestion in *Moses and Monotheism*. David Bakan has argued that Freud's interpretation indicated a way to eliminate Jewish persecu-

15. *Ibid.*
16. *Ibid.* The emphasis must be placed on the word *"forestall."*
17. See the excerpt from Moshe's speech quoted above.

tion. Freud considered such persecution a result of resentment toward the Jew for the moral burden of the law.[18] By suggesting that Moses was really an Egyptian, Freud directed responsibility for the law away from the Jews in an effort to alleviate anti-Semitism. Freud suggested that the Jews could end their identification with the superego by terminating their role as the conscience of mankind. Freud's reasoning is incompatible with the traditional Jewish appreciation of law and with Wiesel's respect for that law. Despite Wiesel's suspicions with respect to the causes of Jewish persecution, he is unwilling to renounce so much of Jewish tradition. He would rather alter the Jewish condition than renounce the thrust of the tradition. Thus, Wiesel applauds the Israeli realization that powerlessness invites persecution, a realization they learned from the horror of history. This lesson could not have been learned had silence been imposed.

In addition, were Wiesel serious about the messianic possibility of silence, the old man would never have been justified in revealing the tale, for the salvation of the world would have been at stake. Furthermore, there is also a fundamental paradox in writing a work that advocates silence with respect to its tale! We may not really know the true mystics. Those whose experiences have come to our attention believe in the word despite their protestations. Suffice it to say that Wiesel does not convincingly argue his case for silence. Rather, he flirts with a romantic possibility.

Despite the fact that Wiesel does not seriously propose silence, he does resolve one of his major problems with respect to the role of witness. By limiting his role to saving another person rather than all humanity, Wiesel defends

18. David Bakan, *Sigmund Freud and the Jewish Mystical Tradition*, pp. 137–168.

the task of witness by endowing it with a mission capable of realization. This limitation coupled with a non-alien, Jewish humanism is consistent with Wiesel's theological vision while it narrows his sociological expectations. It provides the underpinning for Wiesel's affirmation of life despite a reality that merits despair.

In *The Oath* Wiesel moves toward an affirmation of life or, more accurately, toward an appeal to life in the face of death. The old man who narrates most of *The Oath* tries desperately to convince his companion that life is important and that death must be outwitted. For the first time in any of Wiesel's novels, the major narrator clearly advocates life. In *Night* death is the only winner of the war, and the overpowering reality of death leaves the narrator with but the slimmest hold on life. In *Dawn* the dead are ever-present to Elisha, and he never fully accepts the call to life that others proclaim. Love and death are intimate companions, and the cost of life is the death of another. In *The Accident* it is a stranger, Dr. Russell, who fights for the narrator's life. Eliezer, the narrator, recalls, "As for me, love or death. I didn't care."[19] Although Eliezer continues to live, he is torn between life and death. In *The Town Beyond the Wall* the narrator, Michael, is brought back from the brink of death by others. His smuggler friend, Meir, discovers him desolate in the streets of Paris and feeds and clothes him. Later Pedro's affirmation of life supports Michael in his hour of need. In *The Gates of the Forest* Gregor-Gavriel wavers between life and death throughout most of the novel. It is only at the end of the story that Gregor-Gavriel is fully able to accept life and to build for a future. In many of Wiesel's novels death is depicted as a welcome relief from the travail of life.

19. *The Accident*, p. 25.

In *The Oath* death is clearly portrayed as the enemy. The old man does concede that death wins out in the end, but while man is alive death must be fought. The old man said: ". . . the game is rigged since death wins in the end . . . . I made them laugh. Only to have death laugh louder still."[20]

To face death lucidly is one thing, to surrender out of weakness or inadvertence is another. I don't ask you to go back on your decision; I only tell you to act freely.[21]

The old man tries to convince his young companion that "escape into death is more senseless than escape into life."[22] For the old man the solution does not lie in death but in a stubborn persistence in life.

While the old man doggedly presents the case for life, the young boy does not successfully represent a serious alternative. The boy proves completely unable to combat the old man's appeal to life with his own call for the oblivion of death. The old man's victory comes too easily, and the reader feels that the deck has been stacked. Furthermore, the old man's insistence on life is dependent upon a preoccupation with death or upon continual combat with death. The old man can only confirm life by revealing the story of an all-consuming death. It is this deathly tale that convinces the young boy to choose life. In addition, the telling of the tale to the young boy and the transfer of responsibility for the tale robs the old man of his hold on life. Wiesel suggests that the old man cannot live much beyond this moment of revelation. There is thus a peculiar irony behind this affirmation of life. The case for life, like the case for silence, is highly ambiguous.

20. *The Oath*, p. 8.
21. *Ibid.*, p. 11.
22. *Ibid.*, p. 14.

It is clear, however, that Wiesel's shift with respect to the role of witness and with respect to his affirmation of life is sociological rather than theological. Wiesel continues to affirm his earlier theological vision of the void. The old man does not endeavor to defend a meaningful cosmos. Rather, he argues for a more limited choice of life with all its pains and problems. As in *The Gates of the Forest*, there is a major confrontation between a Rebbe and a narrator in which the Rebbe concedes the legitimacy of the narrator's challenge to the theodicy of Israel but argues that the secret must be kept in order to preserve the joy of the community. In *The Oath* another Rebbe says to the old man:

". . . but keep away from my people. Don't associate with them, don't talk to them. Don't kill the joy they believe to have found under my roof; for them it is necessary if not indispensable to preserve this joy."[23]

The Rebbe later continues:

"There is no room under this roof for anyone who cannot control his sorrow and prevent it from affecting his fellow-man."[24]

In *The Oath* Wiesel does not deny the persistence of the void; he only changes his strategy for dealing with it. His fundamental vision has not changed.

Zalmen, or The Madness of God: The Option of Madness

The theme of madness, which is present though not necessarily dominant in the rest of Wiesel's work, is predominant in his play *Zalmen, or the Madness of God*. The play was first published in France in 1968, and the English translation

23. *Ibid.*, p. 38.
24. *Ibid.*, p. 40.

was produced for National Educational Television in the United States in 1974. It has been performed on Broadway and has most recently appeared in print in 1975. I wish to consider *Zalmen, or the Madness of God* within this chapter, which considers Wiesel's recent writings, even though the chronology of its writing (as opposed to its English appearance) would place it earlier. For both literary and theological reasons the work can be grouped with his recent writing. From a literary perspective, Wiesel's recent works have tended to experiment with alternate genre. In *Souls on Fire* (1970) and *Messengers of God* (1976) Wiesel presents a Hasidic and Midrashic collection of tales and in *Ani Maamin* (1973) he wrote a cantata. *Zalmen, or the Madness of God* is another attempt at writing in an alternate genre. From a theological perspective, as we shall shortly see, Wiesel's position strongly resembles the theological position of *The Oath* with its limited task of witness. Similarly, in *Zalmen, or the Madness of God,* madness enjoys only a limited success. It too saves but one person. The grand hope has been reduced to a modest scale.

Following upon *The Jews of Silence* and "Moscow Revisited" in *Legends of Our Time,* this play presents another scenario in the Soviet Union. In both the earlier works Wiesel struggled to describe the reawakening of the Jewish people, a reawakening that is truly mythic in its dimensions, with reportorial accuracy and a sense of balance, tone, and style. In *Zalmen, or the Madness of God* Wiesel abandons the guise of realism and gives his imagination full reign. Nonetheless, the madness he depicts in this play is not unprecedented in his literary corpus.

In *Night* Wiesel described madness as a correct perception of reality in a world gone mad. Only the mad person could truly perceive or express the horrors of reality. Sanity becomes insanity in a mad world. Moche the Beadle, the man who had been to the camps and returned to tell the tale, was labeled mad. Madame Schäcter, the woman on the train who correctly foresaw the flames of the crematoria, revealed a truth prior to its time and was consequently considered mad. The dedication of *The Town Beyond the Wall* begins with the quote from Dostoevski, "I have a plan — To go mad." Again, Moishe appears, and this Moishe knows:

"I'm a madman and in this base world only madmen know. They know that everything is false. Wine is false, the heart is false, tears are false. And maybe the madmen are false too."[25]

Varady goes mad, and his madness allows him to imagine the power to endure and impose his will upon reality. Pedro, Michael's teacher, prays the madman's prayer:

Oh God, give me the strength to sin against you, to oppose your will! Give me the strength to deny you, reject you, imprison you, ridicule you![26]

Pedro's madness is not Moishe's madness or Madame Schäcter's. His madness is not a correct perception of reality; rather it is an act of freedom that allows the individual to transcend his fate and alter his destiny.

In *The Gates of the Forest* the madmen are the pious ones, the righteous ones without whom the world could not continue to exist, while in both *A Beggar in Jerusalem* and *Souls on Fire* the madmen are those who can free themselves from conventionality and create alternatives. In this context Wiesel's madness is roughly equivalent to Marcuse's critical thinking. The madman for Wiesel is the sane

25. *The Town Beyond the Wall*, p. 15.
26. *Ibid.*, p. 48.

man who perceives universal madness. Wiesel describes the famous tale of Rabbi Nachman of Bratslav:

Once upon a time there was a king who knew that the next harvest would be cursed. Whosoever would eat from it would go mad. And so he ordered an enormous granary built and stored there all that remained from the last crop. He entrusted the key to his friend and this is what he told him: "When my subjects and their king will have been struck with madness, you alone will have the right to enter the storehouse and eat uncontaminated food. Thus you will escape the malediction. But in exchange, your mission will be to cover the earth, going from country to country, from town to town, from one street to the other, from one man to the other, telling tales, ours — and you will shout, you will shout with all your might: Good people, do not forget! What is at stake is your life, your survival! Do not forget, do not forget!"[27]

In *The Oath* Wiesel persists in the theme of madness as Moshe returns and suggests an alternative way to route persecution. However, only in *Zalmen, or the Madness of God* is madness the major theme of a work. The limited hope that results from this madness is indicative of the fragile dimension of human hope that Wiesel sees in the world of the void.

The setting for the play is the Soviet Union late in the 1950's after the Stalin era of fear and before the renaissance of Jewish identity and hope. Wiesel traces the source of the play to his experience on Yom Kippur, 1965 in the Moscow synagogue. Wiesel fantasized the Rabbi going mad and thus entering the domain of legend. Wiesel, like Zalmen the beadle in his drama, hoped the Rabbi would go mad by strengthening and freeing his imagination. Zalmen urges the

27. *Souls on Fire*, p. 202.

Rabbi to break the bonds of the conventional and go mad. Like Pedro instructing Michael, Zalmen argues:

And who tells you this is how God wants you: bowed down, begging for punishment and pardon? Who tells you He wouldn't rather see you strong and proud in spite of your despair?[28]
Lose yourself! Shout! Let your call be heard, gather your forces.[29]

For Zalmen, madness is the Rabbi's destiny.

But today may be the day! The day that has been waiting for you and you alone since the beginning of creation. Will you let it slip by, Rabbi? Will you?[30]

The chairman of the synagogue is a Jew who must work both with the enemy against his people, and with his people against the enemy. His argument, as opposed to Zalmen's, brings to bear the whole weight of the Jewish tradition that argued for compliance and endurance rather than risk and confrontation.

That's far enough for me. You know what I mean. You are neither stupid nor naive. We have managed to survive innumerable persecutions over the centuries. How did we do it? We learned to wait, to exercise restraint. Waiting was a necessity for us and we turned it into an art. That required sacrificing certain relationships, certain rituals — so what? We had no choice. Don't you think I too could give up, choose the easy way out and resign? Would that solve the problem? Surely not. Therefore, I say we must accept and endure and — don't be shocked — collaborate. Or at least, play the game of collaboration.[31]

---

28. Elie Wiesel, *Zalmen, or the Madness of God* (New York: Random House, 1975), p. 5.
29. *Ibid.*, p. 6.
30. *Ibid.*, p. 7.
31. *Ibid.*, p. 45.

Wiesel points to the tragic historical significance of this tradition by his conspicuous creation of an alternate tradition, in the option of madness (which the rabbi chooses here), in his challenges to God, or in his general suspicion of authority. The Rabbi is in a quandary. The occasion is the eve of Yom Kippur, his community is dying, and daily they suffer oppression compounded by oppressive silence. Foreigners come to the Synagogue, outsiders, free people. They too are mad, magicians and entertainers entering the Synagogue to join the community in prayer. What should the Rabbi do? Zalmen pushes him toward madness; the chairman encourages endurance. The Rabbi's family considers him a sad vestige. The future is bleak and the present without consolation. The Rabbi's dialogue with a member of the board, an assimilated physician drawn to his Jewishness by the shame of survival, gives a clue to the passion that rages within:

It's all a question of where you place the accent. God requires of man not that he live, but that he choose to live. What matters is to choose — at the risk of being defeated. . . .

Death comes only later; it does not affect the choice itself.[32]

Although the Rabbi hesitates and claims he is too old to choose again, too old to risk, he cannot resist Zalmen's coaxing. The Rabbi fears that he has forgotten; Zalmen demands that he remember:

You lack imagination, Rabbi! You've lost hope. That's bad enough, but worse — you've closed yourself to imagination! That's unforgivable, Rabbi! For we are the imagination and madness of the world — we are imagination gone mad. One has to be mad today to believe in God and in man — one has to be mad to

32. *Ibid.*, p. 53.

believe. One has to be mad to want to remain human. Be mad, Rabbi, be mad![33]

The Rabbi goes mad. The nature of his action, the quality of his madness, is never revealed to the audience who must surmise the Rabbi's action from the various characters' reactions. Their response, however, reveals as much about themselves as it does about the Rabbi. The chairman is concerned with preserving the remnant; the Rabbi must be saved, for he is the last vestige of a former world. The assimilated doctor considers the Rabbi's act authentic, and he courageously follows the foreigners to speak on behalf of the Rabbi and to reveal the bleak situation that drove the Rabbi mad. However, he does not act in time (the foreigners have already left), and thus his action is ineffectual. The Rabbi's assimilated son-in-law, Alexy, finds the Rabbi a pathetic old man, and he resents having to re-confront a past he has renounced. Nina, Alexy's wife and the Rabbi's daughter, feels guilt in her father's presence. She is torn between loyalty to her father and to her husband (who is a communist). The Inspector, the Commissar of Jewish Affairs at the Ministry of Culture, is perturbed by the Rabbi's actions, which represent but one more bureaucratic hassle that he must handle. Only Misha, the Rabbi's grandson, discovers a new dimension to his inner self as he confronts the Rabbi's actions.

The investigator finally resolves the situation bureaucratically. Since the Rabbi's actions create more problems than they resolve, the investigator decides to bureaucratically categorize the act as a non-act. He consequently denies that the action ever took place. He says:

Poor hero, poor dreamer. You have lost and I feel sorry for you; you have fought for nothing. Your offering was not accepted.

33. *Ibid.*, p. 79.

Worse — it wasn't even noticed. . . . You thought their anger would explode and shatter human conscience? Well — it's too bad. . . . Life goes on. And those who don't suffer refuse to hear about suffering — and particularly about Jewish suffering. That is why I pity you. You were beaten from the start, you never had a chance. And now you know it. You know that you cannot count on anyone and, what's more, that you don't count for anyone. . . . As far as we're concerned — as far as the outside world is concerned — you have done nothing. . . . Well, my sad hero, that revolt quite simply *did not take place!*[34]

The doctor understands the cruelty of the investigator. The investigator denies madness its efficacy, its power, its moment of lucid authenticity. Misha, the Rabbi's twelve-year-old grandson, has discovered his love for his grandfather, and as the play ends, the voice of his father calls Misha from the distance to "come back," not to go toward the world of his grandfather. Even though the Rabbi is filled with doubts, Misha has been touched. Madness has triumphed, if only for one person.

As in *The Oath,* Wiesel has narrowed his scope and seeks more limited victories. The role of witness and madness, the moral madness that was to save the world, has had its moment and claimed its moderate victory. One spark has been reunited, one lonely, isolated spark.

Ani Maamin: Theodicy and the Persistence of the Void

Ani Maamin is in many ways Wiesel's most theological work. Commissioned by the Union of American Hebrew Congregations and performed in Carnegie Hall only six weeks after the Yom Kippur war, this cantata was billed as a celebration of the triumph of faith. The setting of the cantata is a dialogue between the patriarchs Abraham,

34. *Ibid.,* pp. 169–170.

Isaac, and Jacob who have been charged with the responsibility of calling God's attention to Israel's suffering. As
the patriarchs witness the Holocaust, they beseech heaven
for a response from God. God, however, remains unmoved.
This beseechment of God by the Patriarchs is in direct
continuity with *Midrash Lamentations Rabbah* (Petichta
24) in which, following the destruction of the first temple,
the Patriarchs, Moses, and finally Rachel are moved by the
suffering of Israel and by Israel's persistent faith. All protest to God against Israel's fate. In Wiesel's representation
and updating of the Midrash, the two radical possibilities
that are found in the traditional Midrash are left out, namely
that the covenant has been broken or that the destruction is
a prelude to the messiah. Wiesel's failure to explore these
two possibilities is important to Wiesel's theological position.

Looking more closely at the traditional midrash,
Wiesel's deviation becomes apparent. The first Midrash
speaks of God,

'He hath broken the covenant': the Ministering Angels spake
before the Holy One, blessed be He: 'Sovereign of the Universe,
broken is the covenant made with their patriarch Abraham
through which the world is peopled and through which men
acknowledge Thee in the world that Thou art God, Most High,
Maker of heaven and earth.'[35]

The same Midrash, however, concludes with the possibility
of hope. When appealed to by the Patriarchs, by Moses,
and finally by Rachel, God yields not with Wiesel's tear of
empathy but with the promise of redemption.

---

35. *Midrash Lamentations Rabbah,* translated by A. Cohen (London: The Soncino Press, 1939), p. 43. In traditional pagination Petichta
24.

Forthwith the mercy of the Holy One, blessed be He, was stirred, and He said, 'For thy sake, Rachel, I will restore Israel to their place.' And so it is written, Thus saith the Lord: A voice is heard in Ramah, lamentation and bitter weeping, Rachel weeping for her children; she refuseth to be comforted for her children, because they are not (Jer. XXXI, 15). This is followed by Thus saith the Lord: Refrain thy voice from weeping, and thine eyes from tears; for thy work shall be rewarded . . . and there is hope for thy future, saith the Lord; and thy children shall return to their own border.[36]

I shall return to these two radical alternatives when I consider Wiesel's work in relationship with Eliezer Berkovits and Richard Rubenstein. For now, suffice it to say that in Wiesel's tale God's response is limited to empathy, and even his tears are hidden from the patriarchs. The covenant is not broken nor is it proclaimed. The promise of hope is not extended. Rather, the proclamation of faith is limited to the acknowledgement that God too weeps even though He does not act and even though his tears are hidden from humanity.

Wiesel's use of the Midrashic mode should not in itself be considered evidence that Wiesel finds the Midrashic viewpoint still valid. Rather, Wiesel's crucial alterations of the Midrash speak of a changed theological vision. Wiesel's use of Midrashic style and his tendency toward mystification have here (as in other works) been misconstrued and his message has been consequently distorted. Thus, *Ani Maamin*, Wiesel's most Midrashic and theological work, may also be his most misunderstood.

The theological question that Wiesel raises in *Ani Maamin* is the question of theodicy. He raises many of the traditional Jewish strategies for defending the plausibility

---

36. *Ibid.*, p. 49; in traditional pagination Petichta 24.

structure of the theodicy and dismisses each of them. The first defense appeals to man's obedience. After Abraham beseeches God on behalf of Israel, a voice responds to him:

The Master of the World
Disposes of the world
His creatures
Do their creator's bidding,
Accept his laws
Without a question.[37]

Abraham, however, refuses to be silenced. He argues that if he had the right to appeal for the people of Sodom, he also has the right to appeal for one million innocent children. The voice responds:

God knows
What he is doing —
For man
That must suffice.[38]

Abraham continues to argue and extracts the promise of salvation, yet even this promise cannot silence him, and he asks the question:

But what kind of messiah
Is a messiah
Who demands
Six million dead
Before he reveals himself?[39]

The voice responds in the spirit of Job's declaration: "The Lord gives, The Lord takes back, May the name of the Lord be blessed."[40]

37. Elie Wiesel, *Ani Maamin: A Song Lost and Found Again* (New York: Random House, 1973), pp. 65–67.
38. *Ibid.*, p. 67.
39. *Ibid.*, pp. 69–71.
40. *Job I:* 21.

. . . God wills,
That is enough.
God takes
And God gives back,
That is enough.
God breaks
And God consoles,
That is enough.[41]

What was for Job an expression of an acceptance of God rankles when it becomes God's self-justification. In its new context these words are an outrage.

Abraham refuses to be assuaged by the voice. Joined by Isaac and Jacob, he argues that there can be no consolation for the Holocaust. The foundation of the state of Israel, the return from exile, the reunion with Jerusalem, the armies and flags are no consolation for the pain and suffering of the victims.

The voice cannot refute Abraham and desperately shifts ground. Rather than defend God, it attacks man for what he has done with God's creation. Although bewildered by this response, the patriarchs do not find it convincing. It leads them, instead, to even greater despair. The narrator continues:

. . . What is the use of shouting that the future corrects nothing? That it is powerless to change the past? What is the use of pleading? The Judge is avenger. There is no hope.[42]

The patriarchs, unlike Job, refuse to be overwhelmed by the voice. They refuse the consolation of the Messiah. They refuse to proclaim the righteousness of the God who murders innocent children. The theodicy of Israel is in shambles. There is no hope. Abraham then suggests a bold new

41. *Ani Maamin,* p. 71.
42. *Ibid.,* p. 77.

path. Humanity must be informed. The secret must be revealed, and the implications of this new revelation are enormous.

Abraham: Their battles will have been for naught —
                    And so will ours.
Isaac: Let us go and tell them.
Jacob: They will die
                    With their eyes open,
                    Facing emptiness.
                    They will perish
                    As free men,
                    Knowing,
                    Aware,
                    They will perish without regret.[43]

The patriarchs have lived a lie. There is no justice, no God who reveals himself through history.

Thus far Wiesel's words are those of a fiery radical who refuses to yield to God's silence. He refuses to be silenced by the voice, refuses to wait for the Messiah or even to accept his coming, and above all, he refuses to compromise with the truth despite its shattering implications. Wiesel then offers a radical vision of God's response to the patriarchs' encounter with the fidelity of Israel. Abraham, Isaac, and Jacob leave heaven to visit their children on earth. They are not recalled by God. The narrator comments: "And the silence of God is God."[44] An analytic philosopher would correctly argue that if God is nothing but silence and inaction, then there is no God. When Abraham descends, he sees women being slaughtered with their children. A little girl who is facing death proclaims: "I believe in you."[45] The narrator comments that, unbeknownst to

43. *Ibid.*, p. 79.
44. *Ibid.*, p. 87.
45. *Ibid.*, p. 91.

Abraham, a tear begins to cloud God's eyes. He does not remain unmoved in the face of such a proclamation of faith.

As the cantata continues, Isaac witnesses the slaughter of the community. On the brink of death its *dayan* (judge) proclaims his belief in God and in the Messiah. God is again moved by this display of faith. However, Isaac, like Abraham, does not see God's tear. ". . . for the second time a tear streams down God's somber countenance, a countenance more somber than before."[46] Jacob witnesses a Passover celebrated in the midst of a concentration camp, deliverance celebrated in a world where there is no hope and no possibility of deliverance. The narrator comments that, unbeknownst to Jacob, "God, surprised by his people, weeps for the third time — and this time without restraint, and with — yes — love. He weeps over his creation — and perhaps over much more than his creation."[47] The patriarchs were greatly moved by their children for their faith in God despite God's inaction. Abraham, the first believer, praised Israel for her faith in God despite God. Isaac, the first survivor who therefore had reason to distrust both man and God, blessed Israel for her faith in man despite man's actions. Finally Jacob, the first son of a survivor, blessed the sons of Israel for their faith in Israel despite both humanity and God.

God does not remain silent for long. Abraham, Isaac, and Jacob leave heaven and, again unbeknownst to them, they are accompanied by God, "weeping, smiling, whispering: *Nitzhuni banai,* my children have defeated me, they deserve my gratitude."[48] The narrator comments:

Thus he spake — he is speaking still.

46. *Ibid.,* p. 97.
47. *Ibid.,* p. 103.
48. *Ibid.,* p. 105.

The word of God continues to be heard.
So does the silence of his dead children.[49]

The cantata concludes with a celebration of Israel's dialectical faith in man and God, despite both man and God.

Blessed are the fools
Who go on laughing,
Who mock the man who mocks the Jew,
Who help their brothers
Singing, over and over and over:
Ani maamin.
Ani maamin beviat ha-Mashiah,
Veaf al pi sheyitmameha,
Akhake lo bekhol yom sheyavo,
Ani Maamin.
(I believe.
I believe in the coming of the Messiah,
and even if he tarries
I shall wait for him on any day that he will come.
I believe.)[50] (translation mine)

Although there is a triumphant tone at the end of the work, Wiesel's bold image of God and his characterization of those who go on laughing as "fools" suggests that the triumphant tone may be theologically hollow. If one may no longer speak of God without speaking of the silence of dead children, one is speaking of a God unworthy of the continuing faith of the Jewish people. It is only God's inaction with respect to His people's fate that belatedly led Him to participate in their anguish. The image of God shedding tears and proclaiming His gratitude is not without strong consoling power. Nevertheless, His tears and His consolation come too late in the cantata. They come after the destruction and

49. *Ibid.*
50. *Ibid.*, p. 107.

only when the victims persisted in proclaiming their faith. Secondly, God's tears are not perceived by Abraham, Isaac, or Jacob, and God's proclamation that His children have defeated Him is also not perceived. Wiesel raises one of the perennial questions of philosophy: namely, whether to be is to be the object of some possible perception. In other words, Wiesel has suggested a majestic, consoling image of a God in tears who is grateful to the Jews for their unmerited faith, yet this image leads us to question whether there can be any difference between a silent, absent God whose empathy is imperceptible to man, and no God at all. Thirdly, the image of God that Wiesel suggests is somewhat pathetic and frighteningly amoral. God has to be shocked into a response, and His response comes too late and is limited to empathy.

The triumphant celebration of faith is theologically hollow. Wiesel's use of "blessed are the fools" suggests that only fools can continue laughing and continue to hope for a messianic future, for such a faith is certainly unwarranted by reality.[51] Despite the tone of triumph, the content of the work is far from triumphant. Despite efforts to rediscover the lost song of *Ani Maamin,* Wiesel has found only the remnant of a faith amid the persistence of the void for he can neither break with the tale and declare the covenant broken nor can he hear the promise of redemption.[52]

Messengers of God: To Begin Again Knowing All

Messengers of God: Biblical Portraits and Legends is Wiesel's representation of Midrashic tales about seven Biblical characters. This work is a continuation of the work

51. Wiesel seems, however, to admire and appreciate that "foolish" faith.
52. See my discussion of Elie Wiesel and contemporary Jewish theology in chapter 7 of this work.

begun in *Souls on Fire*. In both works Wiesel stands as a
teacher and interpreter of the tradition that formed him.
Originally delivered in the form of public lectures at his
popular adult education series given at the 92nd Street
YMHA in New York City, the material was later reworked
for publication. In *Souls on Fire* Wiesel continually undercuts the material to stress both a nostalgia for the past and a
yearning to begin again. References to Hasidic achieve-
ments of near redemption are juxtaposed with the overwhelming reality of death. Rabbis who had crossed the
Polish countryside "raising sparks and kindling flames
everywhere they went" proved impotent as they ap-
proached Auschwitz.[53] Miracle workers failed to work their
miracles, for "Death negates miracles, the death of one
million children negates more than miracles."[54] In *Messengers of God*, Wiesel's mood is less ironic, less dialectical.
Nonetheless, Wiesel still attempts both to assimilate the
Holocaust into the idiom of previous Jewish theology and to
respond to the unprecedented nature of the Holocaust by
transforming previous theology. Wiesel constructs
paradigmatic models based on biblical characters that allow
the individual to begin again and to commit himself to the
future. The urgency of the present and the need to face the
future seem to have tempered Wiesel's earlier vision of the
void or at least his need to expose the radical nature of that
vision.

In the introduction to *Souls on Fire* the story that links
the survivor and his ancestor must bridge a silent storm.

My father, an enlightened spirit, believed in man.
My grandfather, a fervent Hasid, believed in God.
The one taught me to speak, the other to sing.

53. *Souls on Fire*, p. 115.
54. *Ibid.*, p. 37.

Both loved stories.
And when I tell mine, I hear their voices.
Whispering from beyond the silenced storm,
they are what links the survivor to their memory.[55]

In the introduction to *Messengers of God,* however, the
story links directly without a gap. No silent storm inter-
venes.

And so, faithful to his promise, the storyteller does nothing but
tell the tale: he transmits what he received, he returns what was
entrusted to him. His story does not begin with his own; it is fitted
into the memory that is the living tradition of his people.

The legends he brings back are the very ones we are living
today.[56]

The Holocaust still lingers on the horizon of *Messengers
of God* and frames Wiesel's perceptions of past and future.
The persistence of survivors, the confrontation with death,
the specter of total annihilations, these themes remain central in the legends chosen. Only from the vantage point of
post-Holocaust existence can the tales be fully understood
or reunderstood. However, with respect to one Biblical
story, Wiesel's choice of tales shows a note of irony. Wiesel
fails to mention the universal Holocaust of the flood from
which Noah and his family were the only survivors while
almost all the other tales are seen as precursors of the
Holocaust. The Akedah is seen as the precursor of the
Holocaust, the murder of Abel as the forerunner of fratricide, and even Job is seen as a survivor. By avoiding all
reference to Noah, perhaps Wiesel wishes to avoid the
implication in the Biblical account that the survivors were

55. *Souls on Fire,* p. vii.
56. Elie Wiesel, *Messengers of God* (New York: Random House,
1976), p. xiv.

righteous or, more importantly, that the dead were all sinners.

The question for Wiesel is how to begin again. Wiesel sees in almost all the tales not merely the presence of death and the collapse of hope but also the cultivation of the inner resources that allowed Adam and Eve to begin again after their expulsion from the garden or after the murder of their son by his brother, and that permitted Isaac to begin again after Abraham, his own father, attempted to kill him.

Adam and Eve did not give in to resignation. In the face of death they decided to fight by giving life, by conferring a meaning on life. After the fall they begin to work, to strive for a future marked by man. Their children would die — never mind! One moment of life contains an eternity, one moment of life is worth eternity.[57]

For Isaac the issue was also survival. He also knew the inevitability of death; he also experienced his imminent death and lived. Isaac for Wiesel is the paradigmatic survivor. In *Messengers of God* he is the third survivor; Adam and Eve had to survive the realization of their own death, Cain, as executioner, was forced to survive the memory of death, and Isaac faced his own death at the hand of his father and survived. Wiesel does not tell us what happened in the intervening years between the Akedah and Isaac's marriage.[58] He doesn't even speak of Isaac's blindness. Nevertheless, from a survivor's perspective, Wiesel imposes two realities upon Isaac, realities which he clearly imposed upon himself as well. Isaac, as Wiesel depicts him, did not break with society. Instead, he used his pain and his

---

57. *Ibid.*, pp. 32–33. Contrast this passage with Pedro's insight into life and death in *The Town Beyond the Wall*, p. 96.

58. Some Rabbinic Traditions consider Isaac as thirty-seven at the time of the Akedah. According to Scripture he married at forty, and thus we have to account for three years. See Shalom Spiegil, *The Last Trial*, translated by Judah Goldin (New York: Schocken Books, 1967).

suffering as a prayer rather than as rancor and malediction. "He had to make something of his memories, his experience, in order to force us to hope."[59] Secondly, "he remained capable of laughter. And in spite of everything, he did laugh."[60] Clearly, Wiesel is speaking about his own choice in the wake of *Night,* a choice that he restates so often in his works, in the theme of silence and in the theme of witness. Wiesel's Isaac, like Wiesel himself, transforms suffering and uses it as a means to heal his community. He expresses some realities while obscuring others for he realizes that a revelation inappropriate to its recipient is destructive.

Similarly, Wiesel protrays both Joseph and Moses as struggling to affirm life in the wake of despair. Joseph's exile, which led to the redemption of Israel, was caused by his brothers' disruptive jealousy. The reason for the redemption from Egypt, as seen by Wiesel, is that Joseph and his followers had the power to dream without despair and the strength to remain true to themselves. Moses' concept of the sacredness of life led him to oppose God in the name of Israel.

Why was Moses so attached to life, to the point of opposing God's will? Was that his way of protesting heaven's use of death to diminish, stimulate and ultimately crush man? Was it his final act on behalf of his people? His way of teaching Israel an urgent and timeless lesson: that life is sacred — always and for everyone — and that no one has the right to give it up? Did the most inspired and fierce prophet of all wish by his example to tell us, through centuries and generations to come, that to live as a man, as a Jew, means to say yes to life, to fight — even against the Almighty — for every spark, for every breath of life?[61]

59. *Messengers of God,* p. 96.
60. *Ibid.,* p. 97.
61. *Ibid.,* pp. 201–202.

Perhaps no other legend indicates the shift in Wiesel's mood and in his perception of his task than his treatment of the familiar, ironic legend of Moses ascending to heaven and asking to see the future. Moses is shown Rabbi Akivah interpreting the crowns on the top of the Torah's letters and hearing Akivah say of his own interpretation, "this is the Torah as given to Moses at Sinai." At this point the bewildered Moses asks God, "Why didn't you give the Torah to Akivah?" God commands silence. Moses asks to see Akivah's future, at which point God shows him the martyred death of Akivah. Moses protests, "Is this the Torah and is this its reward?" at which point God again commands silence. "This is my will, this is the way I envision things." Wiesel comments tersely, "And Moses kept a respectful silence, just as, centuries later, Rabbi Akivah remained silent on the day when he faced both death and eternity."[62] Wiesel, the master of protest, allows silence the final word. With respect to this legend he embellishes not at all: he changes nothing, adds nothing. Perhaps Wiesel has come to believe that one must accept reality as given and then transform it in the name of life, affirming life in the name of what God should have been.

Similarly, the shift in Wiesel's mood is apparent if we turn to the Joseph story and consider Wiesel's pronouncements against despair in comparison with the old man's instructions in *The Oath:* "I am not telling you not to despair of man, I only ask you not to offer death one more victim, one more victory. . . ."[63] This shift was most obviously precipitated by the Yom Kippur War. Again the sense is not that despair is unwarranted, but rather that the

62. *Ibid.,* p. 176.
63. *The Oath,* p. 12.

consequences of despair may lead to the loss of the ability to alter reality.

Wiesel's accusations against God function therapeutically. Wiesel knows full well that God did not answer Job; He merely overwhelmed him. Wiesel is deeply angry at the manner of God's response. Like those whose concern is with defending theodicy whether or not it blinds them to individual suffering, God ignored Job's personal dilemma.

Actually, God said nothing that Job could interpret as an answer or an explanation or a justification of his ordeals. God did not say: You sinned, you did wrong. Nor did He admit His own error. He dealt in generalities, offering nothing but vast simplifications. Job's individual experience, his personal misfortunes mattered little; what mattered was the context, the overall picture. The concept of suffering was more important than suffering; the question of knowledge was more important than knowledge. God spoke to Job of everything except that which concerned him; He denied him his right to individuality.[64]

Wiesel is unwilling to preserve the sacred theodicy of his youth if its cost is a denial of the individual and the reality of his pain. The defeated Job is not a man Wiesel admires. Wiesel would prefer that Job transcend his weakness and allow his accusations to define his individuality. In his use of Midrash, Wiesel attempts to restore individuality and personality to those people robbed of it by an overwhelming universe. He seeks to teach us to begin again with an affirmation of life despite the overwhelming reality of death and despair.

We have seen, through a detailed examination of Wiesel's corpus, that the theological center has shifted from the once-present God to the human spirit, the communal

64. *Messengers of God*, p. 231.

Jewish spirit that lives with the memories of God's presence
and His radical absence. Thus far, I have chronologically
treated each of Wiesel's works to see how he develops
various themes. In the next three chapters I shall topically
examine three additional facets of Wiesel's religious
thought: his doctrine of Israel, his relationship with contemporary Jewish theology, and his understanding of the
Holocaust.

Chapter Six

The Additional Covenant —
Wiesel's Doctrine of Israel

ELIE WIESEL is no less a theologian of the void with respect to his treatment of Israel than he is with respect to his treatment of God. God and Israel are inseparable according to Jewish tradition, and thus the challenges that Wiesel hurls at God threaten not only to destroy the theodicy of Judaism but Israel's *raison d'être* as well. Nonetheless, Wiesel wishes to maintain the centrality of Israel. He wishes to affirm Israel's sense of mission without relying upon a God who failed His people in their hour of greatest need. Wiesel partially resolves this dilemma through an additional covenant forged at Auschwitz, a covenant that renews Israel's mission despite the void.

Wiesel was heir to the Rabbinic, prophetic, and mystical traditions, all of which posited a crucial relationship between God and Israel. The Rabbinic and prophetic traditions maintained that God and Israel were intertwined in a covenant of trust, fidelity, and protection, a moral covenant that demanded the best of God and Israel.[1] Wiesel's

---

1. R. J. Werblowsky, "Faith, Hope, and Trust — An Analysis of the Concept of Bittachon," *Annual of Jewish Studies,* Vol. 2 (1964).

difficulties with the traditions of God thus entailed difficulties with the traditions of Israel. The Jewish mystical tradition further intensified Wiesel's dilemma by two of its doctrines, the doctrine of *Tikkun* and the doctrine of chosenness.

According to the first mystical doctrine found in the tradition of Lurrianic Kabbalism,[2] Israel was charged with the ontological responsibility for the reunification of divine sparks scattered by the cosmic catastrophe of creation. The doctrine of *Tikkun*, restoration, implies that Jewish observance of the commandments reunites the cosmic sparks with their divine source. According to Gershom Scholem, in the mystical tradition:

Mitswah became an event of cosmic importance, an act which had a bearing upon the dynamics of the universe. The religious Jew became a protagonist in the drama of the world; he manipulated the strings behind the scenes.[3]

According to the doctrine of *Tikkun*, seemingly insignificant acts take on cosmic dimensions in the redemption of the universe. Israel comes to occupy the center stage in the human drama.

The second mystical doctrine contributing to Wiesel's dilemma is the doctrine of Israel's chosenness. Perhaps the clearest statement of this chosenness is found within the Hasidic tradition in the writings of Rabbi Scheneor Zalman of Liadi. Scheneor Zalman maintained that Jews possess two souls, an animal soul and a divine soul. The divine soul is part of the *En Sof*, the *deus absconditus*, whose purpose

2. The dates of Lurrianic Kabbalism are roughly late sixteenth century onward. Rabbi Isaac Luria was born in 1534 in Jerusalem. At his death in 1572, he was head of the famous mystical circle of Safed. His doctrines were made known by his disciple, Rabbi Hayyim Vital.
3. Gershom Scholem, *Major Trends in Jewish Mysticism* (New York: 1946), pp. 29–30.

is to purify the animal soul. Scheneor Zalman believed that only Jews receive divine souls.[4]

Wiesel's early exposure to the mystical doctrines of Israel's chosenness and centrality solidified his estimate of the innate superiority of the Jewish people both ontologically and historically.[5] Wiesel is currently estranged from both the cosmic and ontic dimensions of Israel's mission, but his initial acceptance of such dimensions precludes a sociological solution. His imagination cannot be kindled by the dimension of history alone. He constantly searches for that lost dimension of ontology only to retreat from its implications, for these implications make him painfully aware of the void.

Wiesel partially resolves this dilemma by suggesting an additional covenant forged at Auschwitz. This covenant is no longer between humanity and God or God and Israel, but rather between Israel and its memories of pain and death, God and meaning. The covenant cannot be between God and Israel for God has proved an unreliable partner in the covenantal bondedness. Therefore, if we are to continue as Jews, our self-affirmation must be based on our choice to remain Jews and to assume the past of Jewish history as our own and as in some way implicated in our future. This self-affirmation is a covenant with the past of Israel, with its pain, its overwhelming experience of death, and its memories of God and of a world infused with meaning.

The elements of the additional covenant are threefold: solidarity, witness, and the sanctification of life. I have

---

4. Rabbi Scheneor Zalman of Liadi was the founder of HABAD Hasidism. He was born in 1747 and died in 1812. For a critical discussion of Scheneor Zalman's psychology, see Louis Jacobs, *Seeker of Unity* (New York: Basic Books, 1966), pp. 64–73, and specifically, pp. 67–68.

5. Revealing biographical passages are found in *Souls on Fire, Legends of Our Time,* and *One Generation After.*

deliberately avoided the term "new covenant" not only for its theological implications but also for the implication that a new covenant entails the negation or fulfillment of the old. Wiesel suggests that the threefold covenant is an additional obligation for those Jews to whom the original covenant is still relevant and meaningful. To other Jews, for whom the original covenant is no longer relevant, the threefold covenant can function as the basis for their self-affirmation as Jews.

The need for an additional covenant was precipitated by the Holocaust. For Wiesel, the Holocaust represents a rupture with the Jewish past, a rupture that is theological as well as historical. The Jewish communities that were most continuous with the past, those that had avoided the inevitable secularization following the enlightenment, died in the Holocaust. The magnitude of the Holocaust, its scope and its radical inhumanity, marked the end of both the covenant between people (in traditional language between man and man) and the covenant between Israel and God. Auschwitz was the terminus of a tradition that began at Sinai, and if in the future there is to be a new beginning that can offer some continuity to that tradition of Sinai, it must begin at Auschwitz where both man and God combined to renounce all that had previously been regarded as sacred. All affirmations, all sanctifications of life, all endeavors to begin again, must commence with a realization of the destructive powers of man and God, and of their respective creations.[6]

Theologically, the rupture with the past can clearly be seen in the collapse of the Midrashic framework. Wiesel concurs with Emil Fackenheim that the distinctive feature of all Jewish theology has been the persistence of the Mid-

6. Elie Wiesel, "Jewish Values in the Post Holocaust Future," *Judaism*, Vol. 16, No. 3 (Summer 1967), pp. 281–282.

rashic framework which assumed God's presence in history as well as Israel's allegiance to the original covenant at Sinai.[7] For Wiesel, the most terrifying theological implication of the Holocaust is the collapse of the Midrashic framework. Wiesel cites a midrash that speaks of the difference between Hanukkah and Purim; Hanukkah, when Jews chose military means to defend themselves against a spiritual threat, and Purim, when Jews chose spiritual means to defend themselves against a physical threat.

The Midrash explains this paradox in the following way: The Jewish people entered into a covenant with God. We are to protect His Torah, and He, in turn, assumes responsibility for Israel's presence in the world. Thus, when our spirituality — the Torah — was in danger, we used force in protecting it; but when our physical existence was threatened, we simply reminded God of His duties and promises deriving from the covenant . . .

Well, it seems that, for the very first time in our history, this very covenant was broken. That is why the Holocaust has terrifying theological implications . . .

In the beginning there was the Holocaust. We must, therefore, start all over again. (italics mine)[8]

There are two reasons why the Midrashic framework of covenant and divine presence is shattered for Wiesel. First of all, the traditional images of God relating to the covenant and God's presence become so difficult and torturous when applied to the reality of Auschwitz that we might prefer to abandon them entirely rather than retain them. Secondly, the covenant implies a posture of trust leading to an acceptance of the historical reality as God ordained.[9] If there

7. Emil Fackenheim, *God's Presence in History* (New York: New York University Press, 1969), 3–14.
8. "Jewish Values in the Post Holocaust Future," pp. 281, 282, 285.
9. This attitude of acceptance is seen very clearly in Irving Rosen-

is to be a protest, it must be a cosmic protest, for the major participants in the drama are God and Israel and not Israel and the nations. An acceptance of this framework ultimately points toward God as the principal actor in the Holocaust, a position that Wiesel illustrates as antithetical to the aggressive posture assumed by the Jews in creating the state of Israel.

Theologically, the demise of the covenanted past can also be seen in the emergence of the state of Israel. In *Dawn* Wiesel maintains that the cost of the historical existence of the Jewish people has been the functional death, if not the deliberate murder, of Elisha, the God who is salvation.[10] Israel was founded because man chose to become God, to take his fate into his hands and to grapple with the life and death decisions of historical existence.

The radical break with the past is not limited to religious language but extends to the forms of historical existence. The emergence of the state of Israel brought an end to the diaspora conditions of landlessness and powerlessness,

---

baum's important work *The Holocaust and Halachah*. Two comments of Rosenbaum are striking. He writes that the Jews who observed the Halachah were "able to face life with dignity, death with serenity — and sometimes ecstasy." (p. 8) He also writes:

> Indeed in almost all the halachik literature of the Holocaust there is hardly any attempt at questioning, yet alone vindicating the justice of the almighty. To some extent this avoidance of theodicy may be explained by the apophthegm attributed to the great spiritual leader of East European Jewry, Rabbi Israel Meir Hacohen, the *Hafetz Hayyim* (d. 1933): "For the believer there are no questions; and for the unbeliever there are no answers."

Since Wiesel has emphasized the centrality of questions in Judaism and continually challenges God, it is important to remember that he is as much creating a tradition as he is reflecting one. The normative stance of the convenantal Jew was much closer to what Irving Rosenbaum described than to the Hasidic masters of *Souls on Fire*. The latter were the exception rather than the rule.

10. See my discussion of *Dawn,* in chapter 1.

which had been the marks of the traditional Jew. Wiesel is aware of the dramatic shift in the character of the Jewish people precipitated by their transformation from landlessness and dependence to landedness and independence. Recalling his first meeting with Gad, Elisha recounts:

"I am Gad," he said in a resonant voice, as if he were uttering some cabalistic sentence which contained an answer to every question. He said "I am Gad" in the same way that Jehovah said "I am that I am."[11]

(Perhaps it is no coincidence that the Israeli name "Gad" would be pronounced in Hebrew as the English "God" or the Yiddish *Gut.*) The Israeli, as depicted in *Dawn,* has no need for self-justification, no need to respond in categories that have been externally imposed upon him. He is self-assertive and future-oriented. Gad promises to give Elisha his future almost as abruptly as the Nazis had robbed him of his past. Elisha recalls the stories of Jewish battles and triumphs, which Gad had related to him, and comments:

This was the first story I had ever heard in which Jews were not the ones to be afraid. Until this moment I had believed that the mission of the Jews was to represent the trembling of history rather than the wind which made it tremble.[12]

This transformation from weakness to strength was not without its cost. Nearly all of the Israeli characters in Wiesel's novels are self-assertive and confident; however, they are unable to approach the depths with the author or with any of his other major characters. The rupture with the past is also reflected in Wiesel's fascination with Soviet Jewry and with the secular Israelis, as well as in his own distance from the Hasidic world of his youth. There is

11. Elie Wiesel, *Dawn* (New York: 1961), p. 19.
12. *Ibid.,* p. 21.

always a sense of strangeness in Wiesel's treatment of Hasidism. Although he is attracted to the ecstatic forms of Hasidic celebration and to the authenticity of that world, he conveys a sense of estrangement except during that transcendent moment when the character is transformed by song. The Hasidic world is the world of the past, a world that has maintained its quest for eternity despite the vicissitudes of history.

In contrast to this estrangement, Wiesel is very much at home with those Jews who have unconsciously developed new forms of Jewish life that either illuminate the void or preserve a love for the Jewish past even in the face of the void. His attraction to Soviet Jewry is not only based upon their plight of suffering and persecution (though that would be sufficient) but is more profoundly rooted in his desire to participate in a cultural renaissance of Jewish identity, albeit without a faith in God. Wiesel came to the Soviet Union to witness Jewish suffering. He returned a year later to participate in Jewish joy.[13] In *The Jews of Silence* Wiesel describes what these Jews with so little education have to teach and not what they have to learn. Their persistence as proud, strong, and defiant Jews in a functionally Godless universe allows for his own persistence as a proud, strong, and defiant Jew.

Wiesel is more attracted by the secular Israelis' rediscovery of their own Jewishness in the wake of their historical experience than he is by the religious affirmations of the self-consciously traditional community. In his writings Wiesel captures the sense of history and the sense of continuity that the secular Israeli felt when he experienced the return to the Western Wall as a return to his place of origin

13. Elie Wiesel, *Legends of Our Time* (New York: 1968), pp. 181–197. In this short story entitled "Moscow Revisited," Wiesel's mood and tone differ sharply from *The Jews of Silence* (New York: 1966).

and as a fulfillment of the hopes, prayers, and legacies of past generations.[14] Wiesel is aware that both the secular Israelis and the Soviet Jews will not become observant Jews remaining within the four cubits of the Halachah. Nonetheless, these secular Jews have discovered a sense of the Jewish spirit and are creating new forms of Jewishness that may help bridge the abyss. Wiesel feels a sense of kinship with the endeavors of the Israelis and the Soviet Jews although he charts a different course for himself.

Solidarity

Solidarity is the first element in Wiesel's additional covenant. For Wiesel, the solidarity of the Jewish people is not a necessity turned virtue, but a virtue that is also necessary. Solidarity is a persistent and honored tradition in Judaism. In the liturgy, the Jew recites, "All Israel is intertwined in friendship."[15] The Talmud dictates that Israel is responsible one for another.[16] Beshtian Hasidism, as Wiesel sees it, is founded on the solidarity of the Jewish people,[17] on a recognition of the overriding importance of mutual responsibility. Wiesel follows an honored tradition of *Aggadah* by creating a moral legend out of this solidarity. He claims that the Six-Day War was won because the Jewish people were united as one. The army commander was accompanied by the ghost of Auschwitz. The soldier was buoyed by the volunteer from abroad. In Russia, the Jews gathered together and cast out the informers among them so that they could share Israel's turmoil with a purity of spirit. The

14. He captures this mood particularly in *A Beggar in Jerusalem* but also in two short stories in *One Generation After,* one entitled "Moïta Gur" and the other "Postwar 1967."
15. "Prayer for the New Moon" in the traditional liturgy.
16. Shebuot 39a, see also *Leviticus Rabbah* 1:10 and *Song of Songs Rabbah* 2:3.
17. Elie Wiesel, *Souls on Fire,* p. 20.

Zaddikim all over the world implored God to insure the survival of the State. For Wiesel, these statements are more than truisms, more than appendices to military planning. They are the very reasons why the state of Israel survived. At times it seems that Wiesel has shifted his early sense of omnipotence from the Zaddik or from his own person to the community as a whole. There is an obvious danger involved in this position, for in the historical world, wars are won because of an imbalance of power. However, Wiesel is not a politician. He is a storyteller, and the story he tells of unity is both cogent and mysterious. He argues that if people can no longer say, "In the beginning God created" and must say "In the beginning there was Auschwitz," then they must no longer pray "Because of our sins we were exiled from our land"[18] but rather, "Because of our solidarity we regained the land and were restored to Jerusalem." The psychological potency of these myths should not be underestimated although they should not be confused with military power.

Wiesel's theology must be considered, like much of recent Black, women's, and Jewish theology, a theology of survival. The central question is one of survival. He writes: "To be a Jew, therefore, is to ask a question — a thousand questions, yet always the same . . . Why and how survive in a universe which negates you?"[19] The parallels between Wiesel's questions and the question of James Cone, William Jones, and Mary Daly are striking. For all three theological movements the questions are the same; the concern with theology is more existential and political than it is metaphysical. History assumes a critical dimension and becomes the significant datum for theology because the suffer-

18. This is the language with which the additional service for the three pilgrimage festivals begins.
19. Elie Wiesel, *One Generation After* (New York: 1970), p. 215.

ing community of the oppressed can never be denied, and the significance of human suffering cannot be mystified or obscured. Finally, even the images of God must be altered if such images lead to powerlessness or acquiescence to oppression. Solidarity is the cornerstone for all survival theology for it is the prerequisite for self-reliance.

Wiesel contends that in the face of hostility a minority people must unite. He advocates a plurality of paths within the Jewish community, but dissent can never exclude or endanger other Jews. His emphasis on solidarity at times leads him to distort Jewish tradition. For example, Wiesel takes the Rabbinic condemnation of the wicked son and exaggerates it to the point where it becomes the primary heresy in Judaism.

Jewish tradition allows man to say anything to God, provided it be on behalf of man. Man's inner liberation is God's justification. It all depends on where the rebel chooses to stand. From inside his community, he may say everything. Let him step outside it, and he will be denied this right. The revolt of the believer is not that of the renegade . . .[20]

Projecting the source and the magnitude of his position onto past traditions, Wiesel seeks to create a traditional legitimation for his emphasis on solidarity.

For Wiesel, the solidarity of the Jewish people is based upon their dissent from Western civilization. Wiesel shares with most Western Jews a love-hate relationship with Western culture. Wiesel writes in a Western tongue, lives in a Western country, is indebted to Western thinkers, and writes for a Western audience, yet he is convinced that the Holocaust was proof of the decadence of Western civiliza-

---

20. *Souls on Fire*, p. 111. A similar quote is found in *One Generation After*, p. 215.

tion.[21] Events in the post-Auschwitz world have only intensified Wiesel's sense of the decadence of Western civilization. Hiroshima, Biafra, Viet Nam, and other atrocities have left Wiesel with the sense that the Holocaust has only raised the tolerance level for inhumanity and guilt and has not humanized people by forcing them to confront their demonic potential.[22] For Wiesel, the decadence of Western civilization is its predominant element and the Holocaust its central expression. The Holocaust has forced contact once again with a certain primordial chaos which not only threatened to devour the Jew and his theology, but which further threatens to envelop the entire world in nuclear holocaust. Wiesel considers the Holocaust the crucial event of the twentieth century if not of the entire modern period. The roots of his conviction are both personal and historical.

Historically, Wiesel argues that the Holocaust has precipitated cultural revolutions in Western countries by intensifying the ordinary dissatisfactions and condemnations that the young direct at their elders.[23] Wiesel welcomes the challenges that have been aimed at Western institutions although he is not particularly happy with the form these challenges have taken. The Holocaust has also exposed a raw nerve within Western tradition by exposing the great potential for inhumanity that Western society now pos-

21. Wiesel discusses this theme most specifically in his collection of essays in *One Generation After*. Special attention should be paid to the following essays in that collection: "One Generation After," "To a Concerned Friend," "To a Young Jew Today," "To a Young German of the New Left," and "Postwar 1967." Also see his contribution to the symposium, "On Jewish Values in the Post-Holocaust Future."

22. Again, the parallels between Jewish theology and Black theology are striking, for if we substitute White for Western, the language would be identical with that of James Cone. See Michael Berenbaum, "Women, Blacks, and Jews: Theologians of Survival," *Religion in Life*, Vol. XLV, No. 1 (Spring 1976).

23. *One Generation After*, pp. 203–204.

sesses. However, Wiesel does not offer a sociological analysis of this decadence. He fails to marshal the historical evidence that might best substantiate his claims. Others, Arendt, Hilberg, Tal, and Rubenstein, for example, have also argued for the centrality of the Holocaust as the crucial event of the twentieth century in that it was the final unbounded expression of certain pervasive currents within modern culture whether they be demographic, bureaucratic, ideological, religious, or systemic. Neither does Wiesel offer a social program of reform nor does he suggest, as did the prophets of old, a concrete program of religious repentance. Here, too, in his historical analysis of the impact and centrality of the Holocaust, he is a theologian of the void. He exposes an encroachment of anarchic forces and a collapse of meaning, but he provides no answers and no solutions. He struggles with the questions.

The personal sources of Wiesel's claim for the centrality of the Holocaust reveal much about Wiesel's character. The Holocaust was such a critical experience in Wiesel's life that he is unable to experience the world except through the lenses of that fundamental experience. In addition, the centrality of the Holocaust preserves in form though not in content the centrality of Israel. (Wiesel obviously cannot celebrate the circumstances of this renewed sense of Israel's centrality; However, the Holocaust does put Israel once again on center stage.)

Wiesel also attributes the solidarity of the Jewish people to their alienation from Christianity and Christian civilization as well as to anti-Semitism. He is basically unsympathetic to Christianity and holds Christianity responsible for the choice of Jews as victims. The Christian resentment of the Jew is not merely a result of the alleged act of deicide. As Freud noted, the Jew is equally resented for providing the God who was to be murdered. According to Wiesel, the

Jew is hated for his civilizing tendencies, for his moral conscience, and above all, for his memory. Kalman, the Kabbalist, said:

The Jews are God's memory and the heart of mankind. We do not always know this, but the others do, and that is why they treat us with suspicion and cruelty. Memory frightens them.[24]

For Wiesel "it was useless to cling to illusions regarding the attitude of history toward the people who long ago had attempted to humanize and thereby sanctify it."[25] The Jew is resented for this very endeavor to sanctify life.

Wiesel considers anti-Israel sentiment as an extension of anti-Semitism. The common denominator between anti-Semitism and opposition to the state of Israel (though not necessarily the current government of Israel) is opposition to Jewish history. However, according to Wiesel, Israel is resented, as is the Jew, for the determination to remain moral in a situation that is not.[26] As in his assessment of the Israeli victory of 1967, one suspects that Wiesel's interpretation is mythically potent but politically naive, a potency and a naivety not unshared by many segments of the American Jewish community. Oil and self-interest have far more to do with opposition to the state of Israel than any moral or anti-moral considerations.

There are two basic dangers in Wiesel's position on anti-Semitism. Firstly, Wiesel can be misinterpreted as advocating the innate moral superiority of the Jewish people.[27] However, he might argue that if there is any

24. Elie Wiesel, *A Beggar in Jerusalem*, p. 113.
25. *Ibid.*, p. 39.
26. *One Generation After*, p. 194.
27. In Meir Kahane's discussion of similar themes in *Never Again* (New York: Pyramid Books, 1970), the dangers that are latent in Wiesel's writings become apparent. Wiesel maintains a delicate balance and never appeals to naked nationalism and anti-Christian sentiment

meaning to the moral superiority of the Jewish people, it is earned rather than innate and must continuously be earned. Secondly, Wiesel's notion of the centrality of the Jewish people and his sensitivity to anti-Semitism may cause him to mistake genuine indifference for active anti-Semitism. (The example of Solzhenitsyn's silence with respect to the Jews in Russia might be relevant here.) The survival of the state of Israel is insignificant to many people who consequently prove indifferent. Wiesel is prone to misinterpret this indifference, and his misinterpretation could prove dangerous if it obscured significant political realities.

Wiesel's basic antipathy toward Christianity for its role in anti-Semitism is intensified by his understanding of the crucifixion of Jesus. Wiesel's rejection of that myth is threefold. He argues that by considering the death of the innocent as an atonement for humanity and a prerequisite for salvation, Christians blunt the impact of human suffering. Like Albert Camus, Wiesel fears that suffering can become tolerable as a meaningful part of the religious structure. In *The Rebel* Camus writes: "In that Christ had suffered and had suffered voluntarily, suffering was no longer unjust."[28] Wiesel does not want any solution to the problem of suffering other than the elimination of suffering wherever possible. Furthermore, the suffering of the innocent is, for Wiesel, the central mystery of human existence and a mystery that encourages the individual to confront both man and God. If Jesus of Nazareth is not a God or if his death was not an atonement, then his death must stand

---

within the Jewish community. The differences between Wiesel and Kahane are the differences between a humanist with a definitive humanistic commitment to his own people and a pride in them, and a chauvinist committed to the innate superiority of his own people.

28. Albert Camus, *The Rebel* (New York: Vintage Books, 1956), p. 33.

as a question. We are far more comfortable with a God who suffers than with the innocent and unwarranted suffering of the individual.

Wiesel also rejects the notion of death as ultimate redemption. The difficult choice for Wiesel is life rather than death. It is easy to die. It is far more difficult to live. Wiesel's imaginative contrast of Jesus and the Jewish concept of the Messiah reveals his attitude toward death.

Man is incapable of imagining his own death; he imagines that of his fellow-man. The survivor resents his survival. That is why the Christians imagine their Saviour expiring on the cross. They thus situate him outside the circle of shame; he dies before the others, instead of the others. And thus the others are made to bear his shame. The Messiah, as seen by the Jews, shows greater courage; he survives all the generations, watches them disappear one after the other — and if he is late in coming, it is perhaps because he is ashamed to reveal himself.[29]

Wiesel's symbolic antagonism to the Christian myth is also intensified by the reenactment of the crucifixion which Jews have witnessed. Jews have been killed, the innocent have suffered, and the world is not yet redeemed. By making evil cosmic, we run the risk of becoming blind to the immediate evil that surrounds us.

Any messiah in whose name men are tortured can only be a false messiah. It is by diminishing evil, present and real evil, experienced evil, that one builds the city of the sun. It is by helping the person who looks at you with tears in his eyes, needing help, needing you or at least your presence, that you may attain perfection.[30]

In summary, Wiesel maintains that the solidarity of the Jew is based on a common kinship, a common memory, and

29. Elie Wiesel, *The Oath* (New York: 1973), p. 69.
30. *Ibid.*, p. 138.

a common historical experience. This solidarity is inten-sified by anti-Semitism, by a sense of alienation from West-ern Christian civilization, and by an affirmation of alternate myths and values. Solidarity is a virtue that possesses enormous power and that leads to self-reliance. Wiesel's appeal to solidarity does run the risk of blinding one to the political, class, and religious differences that really divide the Jewish people. Personally, Wiesel sees no conflict be-tween his sense of solidarity with the Jewish people and his role as a man in the world, for only by affirming a particular community can he reach out and embrace mankind. By speaking to his particular community, he speaks to all hu-manity. Ecumenicism when understood as an attempt to patch over our differences in the name of community would be, for Wiesel, a violation of individual and communal authenticity.

Witness

The first element of the additional covenant forged at Ausch-witz was solidarity. The second element is witness. For Wiesel, to be a Jew in the post-Holocaust world is to be a witness, a witness to a sacred past of some four thousand years of history and to the ability to soar to the heights of holiness and descend to the depths of inhumanity. Jewish eyes have seen and Jewish ears have heard the awesome revelation at Sinai and the equally awesome (anti) revela-tion at Auschwitz. For Wiesel, Jewish voices must testify to both moments in human history. It is through this element of witness that Wiesel partially resolves his duties to the past without returning to the world of the past or denying its legitimacy. He preserves a semblance of Israel's mission though this mission is detached from ontological roots.

Viktor Frankl has argued that the chances of an individ-ual surviving the concentration camp psychically intact dramatically increased if his life had a sense of meaning and purpose.[31] Throughout the first part of his ordeal, as depicted in *Night,* Eliezer was sustained by his father, and he sustained his father as well. The relationship of father and son gave him some semblance of meaning in a world bereft of it. After his father's death, Eliezer became apathetic. It was only when he came to regard himself as a witness that he reachieved a reason to live.[32]

For Wiesel, the role of Witness is an immensely complicated one. The struggle is between the impossibility of not bearing witness and the attraction to silence. Wiesel writes:

> For the fact that he has survived commands him to bear witness. But how can he speak up without committing treason against himself and others? A dialectical trap from which there is no escape: the true witness must be silent . . .[33]

Wiesel is frustrated by the futility of the role of witness and intrigued by the possibility of silence; however, at the same time he is convinced that a sacred opportunity to alter the world's relationship to the Jews was lost by bearing false witness, premature witness, or violating the canons of strict silence. In *One Gerneration After* he expressed the fear that words might betray the dead, for words threaten to destroy the mystery behind the experience as well as the immediacy and intensity of the experience itself. Little has been learned if the world has changed so little. The continued persecution of Jews and the persistence of crimes against other peoples led Wiesel to question the efficacy of the role of witness and the ultimate faith in humanity that such a

31. Viktor Frankl, *Man's Search for Meaning* (Boston: Beacon Press, 1963), pp. 70–79.

32. Elie Wiesel, *Night,* pp. 117–124.

33. Elie Wiesel, "A Plea for the Survivors," in *Sh'ma,* No. 100 (February 1976), p. 2.

witness implies.[34] In the *Oath,* as we have seen, Wiesel once again returns to the theme of witness and the tension between silence and witness, witness and guilt. The witness must tell his tale not to save the world but rather to save a single soul.

Wiesel's personal role of witness is twofold. He is both the witness of the Holocaust for the post-Holocaust world, insisting upon a total confrontation with what transpired in the kingdom of night, and a witness to the victims of what transpires in the modern world. He presents the world of the victims to us and judges our world by the laws of the dead.

For Wiesel, the role of witness involves even more than a mutual representation of one world to another. It also involves the telling of tales that would be lost to history without the witness. Eastern European Jewry was destroyed, so if their world is to make some contribution to ours, their stories must be told, their yearnings shared, and their inner resources uncovered. Their memory must be kept alive in order to enrich ours and in order to preserve some sense of continuity with the past. In *The Oath* Wiesel attempts (without real success) to reject this role for the witness.

In the broadest sense the role of witness is not limited to the actual victims or the actual survivors. All Jews are survivors and all Jews are victims. If we follow the tradition of the Passover Haggadah:

In every generation each man must regard himself as though he personally went forth from Egypt.[35]

34. *One Generation After,* pp. 3–4.
35. Morris Silverman, trans., *Passover Haggadah* (Hartford: Prayer Book Press, 1959), p. 28.

then every post-Holocaust Jew must regard himself as
though he personally went into the camps and emerged.
The quality of a person's testimony depends upon the degree to which he accepts this past as his own and thereby
allows it to alter his future perceptions of reality. The
Jewish community has, in fact, been radically altered by the
experience of the Holocaust, and new attitudes and patterns of behavior have been engendered by that experience.
Wiesel details a number of ways in which the Holocaust has
decisively altered (or should decisively alter) the behavior
of the Jewish people and the quality of their testimony.[36]

Wiesel suggests that after Auschwitz, to be a Jew is to
resist fear. Speaking to Barbara, a Parisian prostitute,
Wiesel's character remarks, "I'm Jewish, and that means
I'm not afraid. Fear no longer is my concern."[37] A Jew
must testify to all that he has seen, and this vision forces
him into a domain beyond fear. At the same time, Wiesel
maintains that a Jew must give more credence to threats
than to promises.[38] Wiesel further contends that to be a Jew
after Auschwitz is to be a questioner. In his essay "To the
Young Jew of Today," he explains that a Jew must resist
easy answers and pursue difficult questions.[39] A Jew must
challenge the assumptions of society, must overcome con-
ventions, and must fight against inhumanity. For Wiesel,

36. This shift in behavior suggests another similarity between the
Egyptian experience of slavery and the Holocaust. The Bible lists a
number of commandments imposed upon the Jews because of their
servitude in Egypt. See *Genesis* 47: 45; *Exodus* 20: 2; *Deuteronomy* 5: 6, 15;
6: 12, 21; 8: 14; 7: 27, 11; 13: 6.

The exodus-like implications of the Holocaust would be another way
of substantiating Lawrence Cunningham's claim that the predominant
theme of *Night* is the anti-exodus. His reading of *Night* is thus consistent
with the rest of Wiesel's writings. See Lawrence Cunningham, "*Night* as
Anti-Exodus" (unpublished manuscript).

37. *One Generation After*, p. 131.

38. *Ibid.*, p. 175. See also *Night*, p. 92.

39. *One Generation After*, p. 215.

"The Jew is in perpetual motion. He is characterized as much by his quest as by his faith, his silence as much as his outcry. He defines himself more by what troubles him than by what reassures him."[40] In the post-Auschwitz era, the Jew must choose worthy causes in order to affect a sense of victory over absurdity. A Jew should be ready for the unexpected, willing both to defend himself and to stand up for others. Above all, Wiesel believes that after Auschwitz the Jew must continually tell the tale of the forces that destroyed the old world and the courage that rebuilt the new world.[41]

Wiesel insists upon the pursuit of difficult questions, and thus affirmations are replaced by questions. This mode of questioning is not just a circuitous way to affirm a sense of meaning without confronting the specific conclusions reached or the course that led to the conclusions. The questions themselves are genuine for, according to Wiesel, all that is left after Auschwitz are questions. Wiesel contends that commonality and community are now the result of shared questions rather than answers. When there are answers, these answers are personal. Almost all paths are personal. The bond that can now unite Israel is not the bond of affirmative commitment but rather the bond of shared questions produced by a common root experience. The fact that today the Jew must stand without answers and reassurance underscores the pervading sense of the void in Wiesel's writing. The Jew who once felt trust and fidelity toward the universe must now face a universe of unanswerable questions. All assurances are gone. There are no set answers to be found, no affirmations that can easily be made.

40. *Ibid.*, p. 214.
41. *Ibid.*, p. 224.

Sanctification

The Jew is left to confront the abyss and charged to witness
a cosmic absence, but it is in the depths of this emptiness
that the battle for meaning begins, that the struggle for
sanctification is born. This experience of the depths and the
kindling of the spark of sanctification is described by Wiesel
in *The Town Beyond the Wall,* in his contribution to the
Symposium on "Jewish Values in the Post-Holocaust Future," in *Souls on Fire,* in *Zalmen, or the Madness of God,*
in *The Oath,* and in *Messengers of God.*

It is the affirmation of life and the possibility of human
meaning in the face of the void that I see as the third
element of the additional covenant, *kedushat ha haim,* the
sanctification of life. The term can be used in two different
ways. Literally, *kedushat ha haim* means the sanctification
of life and can signify that the very act of survival is holy.
Quoting a Russian Jewish student, Wiesel writes: "Our
answer lies in the fact that we continue to survive and that
we wish to go on surviving."[42] Survival itself can be a
sanctified response to an inhuman world. Survival is a fundamental act of faith for the Jewish people, our basic commitment to the Jewish future. However, there is a second,
more pervasive sense in which the term "sanctification of
life" can be used, and this second sense most accurately
describes the third element of the additional covenant. In
this sense *kedushat ha haim* entails an endeavor to sanctify
not merely the very act of survival but the quality of that
survival. Wiesel writes of this second sense of sanctification in the traditional context when he speaks of the
covenant that all Jews share:

Are we not brothers in the same ancient tradition, sharing a

42. *The Jews of Silence,* p. 28.

common belief in the eternity of Israel? Do we not observe together the commandment bidding us to sanctify our lives?[43]

Wiesel's Moses in *Messengers of God* tells us what the Rabbi who goes mad in *Zalmen or the Madness of God* also knew. Wiesel's Moses told us:

through centuries and generations to come, that to live as a man, as a Jew, means to say yes to life, to fight — even against the Almighty — for every spark, for every breath of life.[44]

Wiesel's Rabbi on the verge of madness knew:

God requires of man not that he live, but that he choose to live. What matters is to choose — at the risk of being defeated.[45]

In this second sense, the sanctification of life entails the endeavor of Israel to make life holy, to sanctify the quality of human existence. This endeavor began at Sinai and remained within the tradition for more than three thousand years. Wiesel maintains that although the ground rules have now changed and the ontological support for this endeavor is no longer credible, the endeavor itself should still continue. Wiesel is uncertain how it will continue or why it should continue, but if this endeavor to sanctify life were to end, madness would ensue. Wiesel writes:

We have not survived centuries of atrocities for nothing.

This is what I think we are trying to prove to ourselves, desperately, because it is desperately needed . . .[46]

Though the commitment to sanctify life is a positive and hopeful decision, the desperation that prompts this position

43. *Ibid.*, p. 28.
44. *Messengers of God*, p. 202.
45. *Ibid.*
46. "Jewish Values in the Post-Holocaust Future," p. 299.

must not be overlooked. For Wiesel, covenant, chosen-ness, and *Tikkun* are no longer genuinely credible concepts that serve to legitimize the sanctification of life.

In the Symposium "On Jewish Values in the Post-Holocaust Future" Wiesel writes of the role of the Jewish people:

In a world of absurdity, we must invent reason, we must create beauty out of nothingness. And because there is murder in the world — and we are the first ones to know it — and we know how hopeless our battle may appear, we have to fight murder and absurdity and give meaning to the battle, if not to our hope.[47]

In Souls on Fire Wiesel similarly writes: "For whoever creates affirms that the creative act has meaning, a meaning which transcends the act itself."[48] Perhaps, for Wiesel, to be a Jew after Auschwitz is to hope for a Messiah and to work for a Messiah while knowing full well that the hope is for naught.

The dimensions of human aspirations have been scaled down with respect to sanctification as they were with re-spect to the role of witness. Sanctification no longer leads to the messianic event of redemption but is rather a solidar-ity act of an individual and/or community designed to momentarily rout the void. Even the Messiah in Wiesel's later writings is not drawn with such grandiosity but is limited to moments of sanctification.

The desire to sanctify life expresses itself in various forms. It is a desire that permeates the experience of Soviet Jews. Wiesel also considers the establishment of the state of Israel just such an endeavor to sanctify life. He writes:

But Israel, for me, also represents a victory over absurdity and

47. *Ibid.*, p. 299.
48. *Souls on Fire*, p. 31.

inhumanity. And if I claim it for myself, it is because I belong to a generation which has known so few.[49]

For Wiesel, the foundation of the state of Israel was a victory over death, though not an unqualified victory. Israel's existence is also a question. It is a question that the Jewish people ask of their past and of their future even as it is a testament to the durability of the Jewish people. The triumph of 1948 expressed a Jewish desire to create in the face of devastation. It also functioned as a tranquilizer for the conscience of Western civilization. The victory of 1967 was different from that of 1948 even though, according to Wiesel, both battles were fought for survival. Wiesel says:

One does not win battles without paying a price, and it is usually one's innocence. Whatever the triumph, sooner or later it begets conditions which call it into question.[50]

Wiesel is pleased with the behavior of the Israelis and with the relative humaneness of the Israeli occupation although he is displeased that such military measures were necessary to insure the survival of Israel. According to Wiesel, Israel's behavior underscores the continuing determination of the Jewish people to sanctify life despite life's injustices.

Wiesel's reaction to criticism of Israel's behavior in the wake of the Six-Day War illustrates his dual commitment to solidarity and sanctification. Wiesel wears his Jewishness as a badge of justice in a manner similar to the way that James Cone wears his Blackness or Mary Daly her Feminism. Wiesel attacks the moral purity and the shortcomings of Western society and thereby challenges the right of Western nations to act as judges. In order to

49. *One Generation After*, p. 170.
50. *Souls on Fire*, p. 143.

insure their silence, Wiesel, like Cone, plays upon the guilt that Western man feels toward his innocent victims (Jews, Blacks, Indians, and women, among others). This guilt-inducing strategy is employed by Wiesel in *Dawn* although it is only completely developed after the Six-Day War. In *Dawn* Wiesel wrote:

> It's cruel — inhuman, if you like. But we have no other choice. For generations we've wanted to be better, more pure in heart than those who persecuted us. You've all seen the result: Hitler and the extermination camps in Germany. We've had enough of trying to be more just than those who claim to speak in the name of justice. When the Nazis killed a third of our people just men found nothing to say. If ever it's a question of killing off Jews, everyone is silent; there are twenty centuries of history to prove it.[51]

Wiesel views criticism of Israel by Western people as arrogance. He argues that those who were silent when the Jews needed their voices should also remain silent now. Only the Jew in solidarity with his people has the right to demand higher standards from Israel. This right stems from the other commitment of the Jew to sanctify life.

The existence of the state of Israel poses an ideological question with respect to the Jewish past. The foundation of the state of Israel was the product of two conflicting ideologies. On the one hand, the state was born in order to insure a people's survival, while on the other it was the heir to three thousand years of tradition and morality which placed different demands upon it. Ronald Sanders has stated the problem clearly, and his own sentiments mirror Wiesel's. He wrote:

> These questions are ways of stating the dilemma of Jewish his-

51. *Dawn*, p. 29.

tory. Anyone who recognizes clearly what happened to the Jews of Europe during the Second World War, anyone with the slightest knowledge of the long *Leidensgeschichte* that preceded it back through the centuries of pogroms, humiliation, blood accusations and burnings at the stake, knows why a Jewish state must survive. Anyone with a sense of the innate values of Jewish history knows why it should continue as such, why Jews shouldn't simply become absorbed into the existing populations wherever they can and eventually disappear as an entity. But isn't there a conflict of principles here? Are the innate values of Jewish history, the persistent Jewish contributions through millenia to the conscience of mankind, compatible with the Realpolitik of a Jewish state?[52]

For Sanders, this problem must be resolved. It demands the best moral creativity of the Jewish people. Wiesel also sees this problem as the fundamental challenge confronting the Jewish people. Wiesel once hoped for a messianic solution, for a level upon which the questions and the answers would be one. With the demise of this hope, Wiesel substituted the concept of a moral Jewish state and its people charged with the sanctification of life. The fact that this sanctification is difficult only highlights the distance between the contemporary world and the messianic hope. The Talmud argues, "In a place where there are no men try to be a man."[53] Wiesel would argue, "Where there are no gods, man must become God." In the process, man becomes aware of his own humanity and his own fragility.

52. Ronald Sanders, "Israel at 25," *Midstream,* Vol. XIX, No. 6 (June/July 1973), p. 68.
53. *Pirke Avot* (Sayings of the Fathers), 2:6.

Chapter Seven

Elie Wiesel and Contemporary
Jewish Theology

WIESEL has thus far been treated in isolation from other theologians. In this chapter Wiesel will be located within the context of contemporary Jewish theology. His theological position will be contrasted with the positions of Eliezer Berkovits, Emil Fackenheim, and Richard Rubenstein in order to elucidate the nature of Wiesel's thought and, further, to speak to the contemporary theological situation.

The discussion will be limited to a comparison of Wiesel's position with the positions taken by Berkovits, Fackenheim, and Rubenstein for they are the only contemporary theologians who have responded to the questions of the Holocaust with book-length essays despite the fact that Jewish faith after the Holocaust is one of the central questions of contemporary Jewish theology. It was Martin Buber's perceptive essay on the *Eclipse of God*[1] that first raised the theological issues of the Holocaust, but despite his early work and despite Wiesel's novels (five of which were published by 1964),[2] it was only after the 1966 publica-

1. Martin Buber, *Eclipse of God* (New York: Harper & Row, 1952).
2. Elie Wiesel, *Night* (1958), *Dawn* (1960), *The Accident* (1961), *The Town Beyond the Wall* (1964), *The Gates of the Forest* (1964).

tion of Rubenstein's *After Auschwitz* that the implications of the Holocaust became a central concern in contemporary Jewish theology. The daring of Rubenstein's contentions and the reception accorded his work within the Christian community demanded a response from Jewish theologians; both Emil Fackenheim and Eliezer Berkovits have accepted the challenge.[3] The Six-Day War has also raised the shadow of the Holocaust.

Wiesel occupies a unique position of authority to each of these theologians. All three recognize the authenticity of his writings and the integrity of his person. Fackenheim's *God's Presence in History* is dedicated to Wiesel. In the preface Fackenheim writes, "The influence of Elie Wiesel will be obvious to any reader; his writings are forcing Jewish theological thought in our time into a new dimension."[4] To Eliezer Berkovits all of the victims possess a unique and unchallengeable authority. He writes, "Those of us who were not there must, before anything else, heed the responses of those who were, for theirs alone are the authentic ones."[5] For Richard Rubenstein Wiesel is the Job of Auschwitz. He writes:

Elie Wiesel's Job-like affirmation of trust in God after Auschwitz has been met with almost universal respect among those who have encountered his writings or his person. I share that regard. I

3. Fackenheim's response on the Holocaust is best stated in his 1968 Deems lectures given at New York University and subsequently published as *God's Presence in History*. I will rely mainly on that work but will also consider a number of his other essays: *Quest for Past and Future* (Boston: Beacon Press, 1968); *Encounters Between Judaism and Modern Philosophy* (New York: Basic Books, Inc., 1973); "On Jewish Values in the Post-Holocaust Future," *Judaism*, Vol. 16, No. 3 (Summer 1967); "The People Israel Lives," *Christian Century*, Vol. 87, No. 28 (May 1970). Berkovits' response to the Holocaust is best stated in his recent book, *Faith after the Holocaust*.

4. Emil Fackenheim, *God's Presence in History*, p. v.

5. Eliezer Berkovits, *Faith After the Holocaust*, p. 4.

concur in the personal appropriateness of Wiesel's use of the example of Job in order to comprehend his own situation.[6]

Because of the uniqueness of Wiesel's authority and the charisma of his person, an understanding of his theological thought within the context of contemporary Jewish theology is all the more imperative if not all the more difficult.

Throughout this chapter the comparisons with Wiesel will be based on the understanding of Wiesel that was developed in the initial chapters of this work. By contrasting Wiesel with each of the three theologians, a different aspect of Wiesel's thought can be highlighted and the fuller implications of his work can be better understood. I will concentrate on that aspect of Wiesel's thought that a comparative analysis can best elucidate.

Fackenheim and Wiesel: The Revelatory Nature of God at Auschwitz

A contrast between the theology of Emil Fackenheim and Elie Wiesel clarifies Wiesel's choice of honesty and complexity over security and simplicity. Fackenheim's theology relates particularly to Wiesel's notion of the additional covenant, to his attempt to discover new ways to speak about God, and to his depiction of the revelatory moment at Auschwitz. In each case Fackenheim formulates his theology to preserve the traditional theodicy of Israel while Wiesel struggles to represent his experience even at the expense of the traditional theodicy.

Although Fackenheim claims to shrink from Wiesel's comparison of Auschwitz to Sinai, his entire endeavor to preserve the theodicy of Israel in the wake of the Holocaust centers on precisely that comparison. Fackenheim senses

6. Richard Rubenstein, "Job and Auschwitz," *Union Seminary Quarterly Review*, Vol. XXV, No. 4 (Summer 1970), p. 430.

that the critical problem for the believing Jew is to affirm God's presence in history and, more particularly, His presence in the Holocaust. In order to speak of God's presence at Auschwitz, Fackenheim turns to the midrashic tradition, the body of rabbinic legend, myth, allegory, and exegesis which, according to Fackenheim, daringly "affirms God's presence in history in full awareness of the fact that the affirmation is strange, extraordinary, or even paradoxical."[7] Fackenheim distinguishes between two root experiences of the Jewish people: the experience at the Sea and the experience at Sinai. At the Sea Israel encountered God's saving presence while at Sinai Israel encountered God's commanding presence. Fackenheim utilizes this distinction in order to affirm God's presence at Auschwitz. He claims that while God's saving presence was definitely absent in the concentration camps, His commanding presence was manifest. The commanding Voice of Auschwitz said:

Jews are forbidden to hand Hitler posthumous victories. They are commanded to survive as Jews, lest the Jewish people perish. They are commanded to remember the victims of Auschwitz, lest their memory perish. They are forbidden to despair of man and his world, and to escape into either cynicism or otherworldliness, lest they cooperate in delivering the world over to the forces of Auschwitz. Finally, they are forbidden to despair of the God of Israel, lest Judaism perish. A secularist Jew cannot make himself believe by a mere act of will, nor can he be commanded to do so . . . And a religious Jew who has stayed with his God may be forced into new, possibly revolutionary relationships with Him. One possibility, however, is wholly unthinkable. A Jew may not respond to Hitler's attempt to destroy Judaism by himself cooperating in its destruction. In ancient times, the unthinkable Jewish sin was idolatry. Today, it is to respond to Hitler by doing his work.[8]

7. Emil Fackenheim, *God's Presence in History*, p. 4.
8. *Ibid.*, p. 84.

Fackenheim's position is open to criticism in terms of both its internal viability and its external credibility. However, the most devastating criticism results when his work is contrasted with the work of Wiesel. While Fackenheim tries to demonstrate the viability of the midrashic tradition for the post-Holocaust world, Wiesel in his writing, which can in itself be considered a midrash on the Holocaust, demonstrates the incompatibility of previous midrashic traditions with the post-Holocaust world.

The midrashic distinction that Fackenheim suggests between God's saving and redeeming presence is questionable: the actual distinction within the midrashim is not absolute. There is a series of midrashim that emphasize the continuity between the God that Israel experienced at the Sea and the God experienced at Sinai. The *Midrash Tanhuma* comments on the first verse of the decalogue: "I am the Lord thy God who brought thee out of the land of Egypt."

Because the Holy One Blessed be He appeared to them at the Sea as a warrior and at Sinai as a scribe teaching Torah . . . The Holy One Blessed be He said to them: "It is I who was at Sinai. I am the Lord thy God."[9]

This midrash stresses the unity behind the various facets of God and minimizes any hint of dualism. Another rabbinic commentary states that God redeemed Israel from Egypt in order that Israel acknowledge Him at Sinai.[10] It is the redeeming God who demanded acknowledgment and obedience at Sinai. Thus, God's redeeming presence as well as His commanding presence were manifest at Sinai. Another midrash emphasizes not only the continuity of the various images of God at the Sea and at Sinai but also the

9. *Midrash Tanhuma, Jethro* 40: 16. (Translation mine.)
10. *Midrash Exodus Rabbah*, XXIX: 2.

redeeming nature of the revealing God at Sinai. Midrash Exodus Rabbah comments:

Another explanation of the I am the Lord Thy God. It is written, I have declared that I have saved, and I have announced, etc. — . . . 'I have declared' to Egypt that you have fled, so that they may hear and pursue after you and be drowned in the sea, as it says, And it was told the king of Egypt that the people had fled. 'And I have saved,' as it says, Thus the Lord saved Israel that day. 'And I have announced' — to the heathen, for it says, The peoples have heard, they tremble. And there was no stranger among you, because it says, And Moses let his father-in-law depart, and immediately after we read, In the third month. Therefore, ye are My witnesses, saith the Lord, and I am God; hence I am the Lord Thy God.[11]

It seems clear from this midrash that the distinction between the commanding presence and the saving presence is blurred. Here it is the saving God who commands and thus proclaims His presence. Furthermore, the model of a God who first saves (as at the Sea) and then commands (as at Sinai) is not even applicable to the chronology of Auschwitz and the foundation of the state of Israel. Does a commanding God who has not saved have the same integrity as a saving God who then commands? Anyone familiar with Wiesel's writings, especially his early works, knows the debasing images that Wiesel has used to capture the horror of a God who could even have been at Auschwitz, let alone who could have then had the audacity to command. Rubenstein has described Fackenheim's God as a cosmic sadist.[12]

Wiesel shares with Fackenheim a sense of obligation and commandment with respect to the Holocaust, but for

11. *Ibid.*, XXIX: 5.
12. Richard L. Rubenstein, "God as Cosmic Sadist," *Christian Century*, Vol. 87, No. 30 (July 29, 1970).

Wiesel this commandment does not stem from a relationship between man and God or between Israel and God but
between Israel and its memories of pain, suffering, God,
and meaning. Wiesel refuses to base the additional covenant on God's relationship with man for he would thereby be
forced to deal with the nature of a Commander who had
chosen such a moment to speak to His people rather than to
save them. Fackenheim ignores the nature of the Commander, and this failure to deal with Him underscores the failure of his attempt to preserve the theodicy of Israel. Fackenheim's failure also highlights the inherent wisdom of
Wiesel's proposal to base the additional covenant on Israel's memory rather than on God's presence.

Fackenheim preserves the midrashic framework in his
reference to God's presence at Auschwitz; Wiesel shatters
it in his depiction of the revelatory nature of the Auschwitz
experience. When Wiesel draws upon midrashic material,
he often uses midrashic language in such a way as to destroy the midrashic framework. Perhaps Michael Wyschogrod's discussion of Fackenheim's work has inadvertently
pointed out the major reason why Wiesel's understanding
of Auschwitz has shattered previous frameworks and why
Fackenheim's attempt to preserve the framework has been
less than successful. Wyschogrod has written:

Israel's faith has always centered about the saving acts of God:
the election, the Exodus, the Temple and the Messiah. However,
more prevalent destruction was in the history of Israel, the acts of
destruction were enshrined in minor fast days while those of
redemption became the joyous proclamation of the Passover and
Tabernacles, of Hannukah and Purim. The God of Israel is a
redeeming God; this is the only message we are authorized to
proclaim . . .[13]

    13. Michael Wyschogrod, "Faith and the Holocaust," *Judaism*,
Vol. 20, No. 3 (Summer 1971), pp. 293–294.

Wyschogrod's orthodox instincts make him acutely uncomfortable with Fackenheim's separation of God's saving presence from His commanding presence. His orthodoxy also points towards Wiesel's essential dilemma. Wiesel cannot deny that traditional Judaism has always proclaimed God's saving presence; however, after his experiences in the camp and in the post-Holocaust world, he cannot find the belief in a saving God credible. The midrashic framework, which staunchly maintains that God and Israel are bound by a covenant that promises redemption, can no longer be preserved. Although the Jews declared to their Christian neighbors, "This is a world that is not yet redeemed," they also believed that the Messiah would eventually redeem the world and manifest the ultimate triumph of justice.

Wiesel also parts company with some of the commandments that Fackenheim hears from the commanding Voice of Auschwitz. Fackenheim believes that "Jews are forbidden to despair of the God of Israel, lest Judaism perish." Yet in all of Wiesel's work there is a sense of despair concerning the human condition, the ontological foundation of the universe, and the possibilities for redemption. Wiesel's overwhelming despair has not led to either impotence or the death of Judaism. For Wiesel despair is the prerequisite for the Jews' adoption of a revolutionary relationship with both man and God. In *The Oath*, for example, the old man directly responds to Fackenheim's prohibition:

I am not telling you not to despair of man, I only ask you not to offer death one more victim, one more victory. . . . I am telling you to resist . . . Stay on the threshold. Like myself. And like myself you will avenge Kolvillag.[14]

Despair toward his fellow men and toward other nations has

14. Elie Wiesel, *The Oath* (New York: Random House, 1973), p. 12.

led the Israeli to a necessary self-reliance and may provide the only possibility for survival. Wiesel senses that Soviet Jews and secular Israelis may be learning how to become proud and defiant Jews as a result of their despair of both humanity and God.

Wiesel's strength and honesty lie in the fact that he does not shrink from the full implications of his experiences out of a fear of their consequences. Fackenheim's prohibitions against despair with respect to man and God stem from a fear of the consequences of such despair rather than from the inherent honesty of such a stance. His arguments, which end in "lest Judaism perish" or "lest they cooperate in delivering the world over to the forces of Auschwitz," indicate a failure of nerve: unlike Wyschogrod's assertions, the wording of Fackenheim's claims does not suggest "We must not despair of God because that despair is unwarranted" but rather "We must not despair because Judaism may perish."

Rubenstein and Wiesel: The Mystery Maker and the Demystifier

The contrast between Rubenstein's work and that of Elie Wiesel reveals the intensity of Wiesel's Jewishness, the scope of his allegiance in form (though not in content) to rabbinic thinking, and the root of his intense attraction to the Jewish community. Rubenstein breaks with the mythic pattern and the symbolic forms of rabbinic Judaism; Wiesel is unable to make that break. He continues to adhere to the symbolic structure of traditional Judaism even though he radically alters its content.

If the reaction of the Jewish community to Wiesel's writing and person has been one of accolade, the reaction to Rubenstein's work has been one of great personal and professional abuse. Some of his theological adversaries have refused to speak of him by name. He has been maliciously accused of allowing Hitler posthumous victories and of continuing Hitler's work.[15] Even nonparticipants in the theological controversy have been singularly harsh in their assessment of his work. Eugene Borowitz, perhaps the most level-headed and tolerant of contemporary Jewish theologians, considers Rubenstein's work a tragic disaster.[16]

Jacob Neusner has pointed out that this abuse is the highest possible tribute to the importance of Rubenstein's work. He writes:

Rubenstein's response to the Holocaust has been searching and courageous. He has raised the difficult questions and responded with painful honesty. The consequence has been an unprecedented torrent of personal abuse, so that he has nearly been driven out of Jewish public life . . . The abuse to which he has been subjected seems to me the highest possible tribute on the part of his enemies to the compelling importance of his contribution.[17]

What then has Rubenstein said? He has argued that after Auschwitz the belief in a redeeming God who is active in history and who will redeem mankind from its vicissitudes is no longer possible. Belief in such a God and an allegiance to the rabbinic theodicy that attempted to justify Him would

15. This accusation was made by Lou H. Silberman ("Concerning Jewish Theology in North America: Some Notes on a Decade," *American Jewish Yearbook*, LXX [1969], p. 57), who follows Fackenheim's claim (see *God's Presence in History*, p. 30) to its logical conclusion. If Rubenstein's writings despair of the God of Israel and if all who despair of the God of Israel offer Hitler a posthumous victory, then Rubenstein is offering Hitler another posthumous victory. Eliezer Berkovits argues in a similar vein in *Faith after the Holocaust*, p. 72.

16. Eugene Borowitz, "Covenant Theology — Another Look, "*World View*, Vol. 16, No. 3 (March 1973), p. 27.

17. Jacob Neusner, "The Implications of the Holocaust," *Journal of Religion*, Vol. 53, No. 3 (Summer 1973), p. 298.

imply that Hitler was part of a divine plan and that Israel was being punished for her sins:

> To see any purpose in the death camps, the traditional believer is forced to regard the most demonic, antihuman explosion in all history as a meaningful expression of God's purposes. The idea is simply too obscene for me to accept.[18]

Rubenstein does not simply suspend judgment concerning God's behavior; he also rejects the rabbinic God. His rejection, however, does not entail an end to religion or an end to Judaism, for in a meaningless world human community becomes all the more important. He writes:

> I have suggested that Judaism is the way in which we share the decisive times and crises of life through the traditions of our inherited community. The need for sharing is not diminished in the time of the death of God. We no longer believe in the God who has the power to annul the tragic necessities of existence; the need to religiously share that existence remains.[19]

Consequently, Rubenstein emphasizes the importance of rituals, rites of passage, and religious community over doctrine and ethics — a priestly rather than prophetic understanding of religion.

Rubenstein's "death of God" differs significantly from that of contemporary Christian theologians, although both Berkovits and Fackenheim seek to force him into the Christian camp and then attack him there.[20]

---

18. Richard L. Rubenstein, *After Auschwitz* (Indianapolis: Bobbs-Merrill Company, Inc. 1966), p. 153.

19. *Ibid.*, pp. 153–154.

20. For Fackenheim's discussion of the death of God see *God's Presence in History*, pp. 49–61. Berkovits' discussion is in *Faith after the Holocaust*, pp. 50–58. Berkovits is particularly unconvincing when he deals with the tragic nature of existence. His criticism of Protestant death-of-God optimism resembles Rubenstein's criticism of Harvey Cox in *After Auschwitz*, pp. 191–207.

The "death of God" for Rubenstein is a cultural phenomenon. He writes:

I believe the most adequate theological description of our times is to be found in the assertion that we live in the time of the death of God. The vitality of death-of-God theology is rooted in the fact that it has faced more openly . . . the truth of the divine-human encounter in our times. The truth is that it is totally non-existent. Those theologies which attempt to find the reality of God's presence in the contemporary world manifest a deep insensitivity to the art, literature, and technology of our times.[21]

For Rubenstein Jewish consciousness of the death of God does not involve a triumphant exultation or a glorious freedom. The death of God is rooted in the impossibility of affirming His presence after Auschwitz. Rubenstein parts company with many of his Christian contemporaries over precisely this issue of the vision that results from the death of God. Whereas many Christian theologians celebrate man's coming of age in the face of the death of God, Rubenstein bemoans the more tragic implications of the death of hope.[22] I do not want to deal at length with Rubenstein's assertion that "omnipotent nothingness is the Lord of all creation"[23] except to state that while its roots can be traced back to Lurianic Kabbalism, they can also be linked to both Hegel and Freud.[24]

Throughout this work Elie Wiesel has been understood as theologian of the void, that is as a theologian who both describes and understands the shattering impact that Auschwitz has had upon Jewish tradition and the possibility of Jewish belief. The view maintained in this work places

21. *After Auschwitz,* pp. 245–246.
22. *Ibid.,* pp. 152–153, 184, 193.
23. *Ibid.,* pp. 154, 225. Richard Rubenstein, *Morality and Eros* (New York: McGraw-Hill Book Co., 1970), pp. 183–197.
24. *After Auschwitz,* p. 219.

Wiesel in substantive agreement with Rubenstein on many important theological issues. Both Wiesel and Rubenstein concur in their assessment of the importance of the Holocaust;[25] they agree on its shattering impact and understand the difficulty of speaking of God after Auschwitz. Both have challenged the theodicy of Israel while stressing the importance of the human community and the priestly functions of religion.[26] Both share a tragic vision, which they have arrived at as a result of their individual experiences with the unjustifiable death of the innocent.[27] Both see the foundation of the state of Israel as the most positive factor in recent Jewish life while recognizing the degree to which the foundation of this state is a rejection of the saving God of Israel.[28] Why, then, has the community treated Rubenstein with such abuse while responding so positively to Wiesel?

The answer may lie in Wiesel's innate "Jewishness" and in his penchant for mystification as opposed to Rubenstein's detachment and his persistent demystification.[29] In a

25. In *After Auschwitz,* p. x, Rubenstein writes: "Although Jewish history is replete with disaster, none has been so radical in its total import as the Holocaust. Our images of God, man and the moral order have been permanently impaired. No Jewish theology will possess even a remote degree of relevance to contemporary Jewish life if it ignores the question of God and the death camps." The similarity to Wiesel is obvious.

26. See the discussion of Gregor's encounter with the Rebbe in Wiesel's *The Gates of the Forest.* Rubenstein insists on the priestly function of religion in *After Auschwitz,* especially in pp. 93–111. The radical difference of terminology between Rubenstein and Wiesel need not obscure the similarity of their orientation.

27. Richard L. Rubenstein, *My Brother Paul* (New York: Harper & Row, 1972), pp. 1–40.

28. See Rubenstein's article on the "Rebirth of Israel in Contemporary Jewish Theology," in *After Auschwitz,* pp. 131–145.

29. The use of mystification and demystification in this book relies heavily upon Peter Berger's understanding of the terms. According to Berger mystification is part of "the falsification of consciousness wherein

perceptive essay entitled "Religious Authority and Mysticism,"[30] Gershom Scholem traces the relationship between religious authority and the mystic, pointing out that there is often a conflict between those who seek to defend and preserve the authority of the tradition and the one who relies upon the authority of his own encounter with the divine. The conflict between the defenders of religious authority and the mystic is mediated in many cases by a number of important factors. Firstly, the mystic is often reared within a specific tradition, so that when he tries to give form to his experience, he tends to use the prevailing symbols and imagery of that tradition. Thus, the imagery that a Roman Catholic uses to articulate his experience will tend to be profoundly Christian while the imagery that a Jew uses will tend to be profoundly Jewish. Scholem cautions that "the exceptions seem to be limited to modern times, with the dissolution of all traditional ties."[31] Secondly, many mystics tend to be conservative, for within their experience they rediscover the root of the authority of the tradition. This conservatism is often insured by the restrictions that a tradition places upon the initiate mystic and by the presence of a guide or guru who can prescribe boundaries for the experience. Thirdly, even in some cases of radical mystical experience, the mystic tends to couch his expression of the experience within the symbolic language of the community by deepening or extending traditional lines of interpretation. He may also give a radically new meaning to the tradition, but even in this covert way he

---

the socio-cultural world which is an edifice of human meanings is overlaid with mysteries posited as non-human in their origins" (*The Sacred Canopy*, p. 90). Demystification is the process of bringing the human origin of humanly created meanings to consciousness.

30. Gershom Scholem, *On the Kabbalah and Its Symbolism* (New York: Schocken Books, 1965), pp. 5–32.

31. *Ibid.*, pp. 5–6.

seems to recognize the tradition's validity by testifying to the continued viability of its symbols. Although Scholem cites a number of other ways in which the mystic either mediates or accentuates his differences with religious authority, these three examples will suffice for an understanding of the conflict between Rubenstein and the established Jewish community and of the acceptance accorded Wiesel.

One need not argue for the mystical nature of either the experiences or the theologies of Richard Rubenstein or Elie Wiesel, for what Gershom Scholem has described with respect to the relationship of the mystic and the established religious authority is equally true of all those who oppose religious authority on the basis of their own individual experience. Both Rubenstein and Wiesel stress the authority of their own experiences, which in both instances were historical rather than mystical. Wiesel's work reflects his fidelity to his own experience and attempts to give it form. Rubenstein writes of his own endeavors:

The theologian is really closer to the poet or the creative artist than to the physical scientist. The value of an artistic creation lies in the fact that a man with a highly sensitive subjectivity is able to communicate something of his own experience which other men recognize as clarifying and enriching their own insights. The theologian, no matter how ecclesiastically oriented he may seem to be, is in reality communicating an inner world he suspects others may share.[32]

It is consistent with Rubenstein's subjective perspective that one of his most recent works is an autobiography and that some of his most perceptive work has been autobiographical in origin.[33]

32. *After Auschwitz*, p. 246.
33. Richard L. Rubenstein, *Power Struggle* (New York: Charles Scribner's Sons, 1974); *My Brother Paul* (New York: Harper & Row,

Wiesel has said of his role as storyteller: "he [the storyteller] has but one motivation: to tell of himself while telling of others."[34]

Scholem's categories may provide new insight into the differences between Wiesel and Rubenstein and into the Jewish community's responses to these very similar theologies. Wiesel was born into the Jewish community and reared according to its traditions. His language, his symbol set, and his mythic structure are all profoundly Jewish. Thomas Indinopulos, a Christian, understands Wiesel's essential Jewishness far better than does Maurice Friedman, a Jew. Indinopulos disputes Friedman's universalistic understanding of Wiesel as a modern Job.[35] Wiesel writes from within the Jewish mythic tradition; his images of God are often re-understandings of traditional images and frequently take the structural and linguistic forms of midrashic exegesis. Wiesel speaks of the Holocaust in terms of the Akedah and of Job. His writing is solidly rooted in Jewish imagery and idiom, and even his sense of the failure of the tradition is expressed in very traditional language. He compares Auschwitz to Sinai; although the covenant established at Sinai has been shattered, he continues to use the language of Sinai and covenant to express that shattering.

Rubenstein, on the other hand, is more of an outsider. Though born to Jewish parents, he was given little Jewish background and came to Judaism of his own choice. He was reared within a different conceptual tradition and writes with equal ease of Freud and Hegel, Melville and Joyce, or

---

1972); "A Rabbi Dies," in Jacob Neusner, *American Judaism* (Englewood Cliffs: Prentice-Hall, 1972), pp. 46–59.

34. *Souls on Fire*, p. 259.

35. Maurice Friedman, *To Deny Our Nothingness*, and Thomas Indinopulos, "The Holocaust in the Stories of Elie Wiesel," *Soundings*, Vol. 55, No. 2 (Summer 1972).

Nietzsche and Kierkegaard. It is through the lenses of other conceptual systems that he comes to write of Auschwitz and Sinai, of covenant and of midrash. Rubenstein is an outsider who has entered a tradition and he evaluates it by external categories. Therefore, unlike Wiesel, he denies the tradition its ultimate authority. His experiences have not allowed him to bow to established authority nor has his work enhanced the mythic and symbolic system itself.

Rubenstein's avid Zionism has not been able to mediate his relationship with the Jewish community. It is interesting to note that even areas of substantive agreement with respect to what may be the central concern of the community cannot override his rejection of Jewish forms. It seems that the authority of the forms speaks louder than the content. While most critics of the state of Israel, such as students, New Leftists, or Christian leaders, have been treated with disdain and anger by the Jewish community, no such response has greeted Jews who have criticized Israel by appealing to the prophetic tradition and to the traditional Jewish sympathy with the underdog. These critics have preserved the mythic structure of the community and the authority of the tradition even while they threaten its most basic interest. The impact of their criticism has been softened by the fact that they implicitly recognize that authority. Both Rubenstein and Wiesel say very similar things with reference to the state of Israel, but they say them in different "languages," and the community is often as sensitive to these languages as to the meaning of the words.

Rubenstein's persistent demystification can best be seen in his writings on the chosenness of Israel and on rabbinic myth. In his article "The Dean and the Chosen People" in *After Auschwitz* Rubenstein argues that the Jew's self-conception of his chosenness has been a significant contributory factor in the Christian's mythical understanding of the Jew as Christ-killer. Rubenstein refuses to use Christian persecutions of Jews as proof of Jewish superiority or chosenness, as both Berkovits and Wiesel are prone to do.[36] Instead, he suggests that both Jew and Christian demystify their views of themselves and hence their views of each other. Unlike other contemporary Jewish theologians, Rubenstein will not exonerate Jews from their responsibility for the way in which Christians see Jews and attempt to combat Judaism:

Can we really blame the Christian community for viewing us through the prism of a mythology of history when we were the first to assert this history of ourselves? As long as we continue to hold to the doctrine of the election of Israel, we will leave ourselves open to the theology expressed by Dean Gruber, that because the Jews are God's Chosen People, God wanted Hitler to punish them.

. . . Religious uniqueness does not necessarily place us at the center of the divine drama of perdition, redemption, and salvation for mankind. All we need for a sane religious life is to recognize that we are, when given normal opportunities, neither more nor less than any other men, sharing the pain, the joy, and the fated destiny which Earth alone has meted out to all her children.[37]

Rubenstein is quite pragmatic. Since Jews are unable to control Christians' conceptions of Judaism, they can at least alter their own self-conceptions of Judaism and thus

36. See *Faith After the Holocaust,* pp. 114–120. On p. 117 Berkovits writes: "The metaphysical quality of the Nazi-German hatred of the Jews as well as the truly diabolical, super-human quality of the Nazi-German criminality against the Jews are themselves testimonies to the dark knowledge with which the Nazified Germany sensed the presence in history of the hiding God." Wiesel speaks to this issue in *One Generation After,* pp. 196–197.

37. Unlike Berkovits, Wiesel refuses to glorify martyrdom. Nevertheless, he also refuses to speak of the Jews in the radically demystified terms of Rubenstein (*After Auschwitz,* p. 58).

demystify at least one part of a rather tense and confused relationship. His claim that "Jews, when given normal opportunities, are neither more nor less than other men" is a clear expression of the intensity of his desire for demystification. Unlike Mordecai Kaplan, Rubenstein does not proceed from a literal rejection of chosenness to a series of claims for Jewish moral superiority, a more acceptable way of claiming chosenness.[38] Rather, he seeks a situation of normalcy: Jews are men like other men, no more and no less.

This same desire for demystification is also clear in Rubenstein's treatment of rabbinic myth and legend in *The Religious Imagination*. Methodologically, Rubenstein's analysis of rabbinic legend is based upon his conviction that religious belief and practice are related to the basic needs "of the human body as it is nurtured within the family and the larger society."[39] The basic needs of the rabbinic Jew were influenced by his situation of landlessness and powerlessness, expressed most clearly in the compensatory dominance of masculinity within rabbinic tradition. Rubenstein refuses to argue for or against the veracity of the rabbinic roles for the sexes. He speaks instead of the functional or dysfunctional nature of these beliefs, given their sociological milieux. Rubenstein argues:

There was an enormous overestimation of the status and the prerogative of the male throughout Rabbinic Judaism. The reasons for this must have been extremely complex. No explanation which fails to include the stresses of defeat, conquest, and minority status upon male Jews will have any degree of adequacy . . . Jewish men lacked the capacity to defend or assure possession of

38. The root of Kaplan's problem with chosenness is not with the results but rather with the idea of a God who chooses. Kaplan does argue for the superiority of Jewish teaching.
39. Richard L. Rubenstein, *The Religious Imagination*, p. xiii.

their own women . . . The Jew reacted to the external threat to his masculinity by asserting it with extra insistence within his own community.[40]

This analysis robs the Rabbis of their aura of absolute authority and reveals them as men valiantly and successfully struggling to preserve themselves psychically under conditions of impotence and military defeat. Thus the reader sees the uniqueness of their authority denied even while becoming aware of the psychological wisdom of their adaptive responses to a difficult reality.

Wiesel's penchant for mystification is so apparent throughout all his works that it hardly needs documentation here. Suffice it to say that such mystification is particularly in evidence in his treatment of Hasidism, his understanding of the Holocaust, his portrayal of his own origins, his reporting of the status of Soviet Jewry, and his writings on the Six-Day War. (His own use of mystification elicits a corresponding reaction in the American Jewish community, which has acted towards Wiesel at times like the admirers of a Hasidic rebbe.)

In summary, the comparison between the writings of Elie Wiesel and Richard Rubenstein reveals Wiesel's innate Jewishness and the manner in which he reaffirms the validity of the symbolic traditions of Judaism by testifying to their viability in handling new dimensions of reality. A consideration of the way in which the community has responded to both men despite the similarities of their theological perceptions forces one to conclude that the Jewish community may be far more sensitive to the forms of theology than to its content: the form of Wiesel's theology is authentically Jewish while the content of his theology exhibits a significant break from the past.

40. *Ibid.,* p. 52.

Berkovits and Wiesel: The Painful Vision of Honesty

A comparison between Wiesel's writings and those of Eliezer Berkovits provides a renewed understanding of Wiesel's compelling honesty as a writer, a new appreciation for his existential agony as a survivor, and an intensified awareness of his distance from the traditional theodicy of Israel with respect to the doctrines of God and Israel. Unlike either Rubenstein or Fackenheim, Eliezer Berkovits is traditional in background and upbringing as well as in thought and practice. He is a distinguished Talmudist and well-versed in medieval Jewish philosophy. His major work on the Holocaust, *Faith after the Holocaust,* is an important response by a recognized orthodox theologian to the challenges posed by the Holocaust.

After an overly long and superfluous beginning,[41] Berkovits presents a lucid and eloquent defense of the traditional theodicy of Israel. Berkovits argues that the correct question to ask after the Holocaust is not "Where was God?" but "Why was there man?" He restates a Talmudic view (it is inaccurate to call it the Talmudic view) that God gave man a radical freedom which often proves dangerous to the very survival of mankind:

The question as to God's presence in history is raised on the assumption that the fear of God ought to protect God's people. The answer is based on a radical redefinition of the concepts of fear and might of God . . . Man can only exist because God

41. Berkovits begins by recounting the failure of Western civilization. He then denounces the ecumenical movement and the naive optimism of "death of God" theology. He is unoriginal in each of his three contributions: Arthur Morse's *While Six Million Died* is far more indicting of Western civilization, Joseph Baer Soloveichik's "Confrontations" *(Tradition)* is an original theological denunciation of ecumenicism, and Richard Rubenstein's critique of Harvey Cox in *After Auschwitz* is a far more powerful response to the optimism of "death of God" theology. This beginning tends to detract from Berkovits' brilliant, original contribution in the second half of *Faith after the Holocaust.*

renounces the use of power on him. This, of course, means that God cannot be present in history through manifest material power. Such presence would destroy history. History is the area of human responsibility and its product.[42]

This understanding of human freedom can lead to a new interpretation of God's omnipotence, as expressed in the midrashic saying, "Who is like You, our God, among the Gods? Who is like You, long suffering in silence?" According to Berkovits, "God is mighty for He shackles His omnipotence and becomes 'powerless' so that history may be possible."[43] However, Berkovits does want to assert God's presence in history as well as His absence so that "man may not perish in the tragic absurdity of his own making."[44] According to Berkovits, God's presence is manifest in His people. Israel bears witness to it by her survival and thereby testifies to a triumph of spirit over the temporality of materialistic civilization.

Berkovits also cites a rabbinic example to speak of Israel's ontological responsibility for the survival of the world. Berkovits retells a Talmudic story in which, upon witnessing the martyrdom of Rabbi Ishmael, the angels in heaven cry out:

'Is this then the Torah? And this its reward?' Whereupon a heavenly voice was heard: 'If I hear another sound, I shall turn the world back to water and my throne's footstool [i.e. the earth] to tohu vabohu. This a decree [gezeirah] from before me. Accept it ye who find your pleasure in the Law, which precedes the creation.

. . . Vabohu! The martyrs, Rabbi Akiba and his saintly friends, did not speak that condemning No. They knew that the real issue

42. Eliezer Berkovits, *Faith after the Holocaust*, pp. 108–109.
43. *Ibid.*, p. 109.
44. *Ibid.*, p. 107.

was not their suffering; at stake was God's act of creation, his freedom and authority to say, "Let there be!" The chosen ones know that the choice is between tohu vabohu of non-existence and their acceptance of the yoke of the divine experiment of creation. Without their acceptance, the world would indeed have to be turned back into nothingness. Only when the chosen ones choose to accept 'the decree' does the world acquire the moral right to continue to exist. As they accept the yoke, God may go on being longsuffering with the rest of mankind.[45]

Berkovits valiantly proposes the notion of radical freedom to account for the suffering and the martyrdom of the Jews. He sees Jewish martyrdom as an expression of Jewish assumption of responsibility, as a sign of Jewish chosenness. The difficulty in this position is most apparent in his writings on *galut* (exile). Berkovits considers *galut* in an almost Rosenzweigian sense as essential to the mission of the Jewish people. Unlike Hegel, who bemoaned the wanderings of the Jews and the inability of Abraham to find a home,[46] Berkovits celebrates such wanderings and endows them with a moral character. Abraham went into exile "because in the world as it existed then Abraham could not find a home."[47] The exile after the year 70 C.E. was a "natural occurrence . . . for in the world as it existed then, a world ruled by the Roman Empire, there was indeed no room for the people of the prophets, for the people of a Hillel and a Rabban Gamaliel."[48] The moral burden to bear witness to God unfortunately involves the choice of exile. Berkovits mistakenly extends this concept of exile to include the current situation of the state of Israel. He writes,

45. *Ibid.*, p. 125.
46. G. W. F. Hegel, *The Spirit of Christianity* [in T.M. Knox], trans. G. W. F. Hegel, *Early Theological Writings* (Chicago: The University of Chicago Press, 1948), p. 185.
47. *Faith after the Holocaust*, p. 122.
48. *Ibid.*, p. 123.

and I quote him in full to avoid any possible misrepresentation:

However, our strength can only come from an understanding of our role in history and our willingness to accept it. The Jewish people and, together with them the state of Israel, are isolated in the world. Certainly among the mighty and powerful they have hardly any reliable friends. But if at this stage of human civilization it were otherwise, they would not be Jewish. If any of the great powers would pour as many airplanes, weapons, and as much manpower assistance into the state of Israel — half as much and half as generously — as Russia does in the case of Egypt, Israel would have entered power history. It would be a minor accessory to it. But Israel does not have the oil resources, the vast territories, the population masses, the strategic position to render it a factor in power history. That is why it is Israel. As a state, Israel is in exile in power history just as Jews as a scattered people were in exile in "the wilderness of the nations." Israel's strength must come from the same resources from which the survival power of the Jew came in the past — from within the Jewish people, from the spirit within the Jew, from his heart and mind. The relative isolation of the state of Israel in the international game of power politics is a natural phenomenon. Even though little Israel has been surprisingly effective in war, what does it amount to in the present-day power constellation? Even as a state, Israel lives in faith history. Such is the spirit of its people.[49]

But Berkovits has seriously misunderstood the current reality of the State of Israel. First of all, Israel has entered the domain of power history. Although this entrance into power history may portend its ultimate demise, it also provides the only possible assurance for survival. Berkovits's claim seems particularly naive, distorted, and dangerous after 1967 when the Israeli army occupied Arab lands and

49. *Ibid.*, p. 164.

extended its territory by military power, and after the Yom
Kippur War when the Russian threat of intervention and the
threat of Israel's nuclear arsenal confirmed Israel's role in
power history. Although there is some credibility to Berkovits's claim that the state of Israel is in exile, it is not in
exile with respect to power history. Its exile — that is, its
relative isolation from the rest of the world — and its
dependence on the superpowers is most regrettable and
must, if possible, be altered. Such exile is certainly not
laudable. Berkovits generally praises powerlessness and
transforms a regrettable state of affairs into an ideology.

Berkovits is perceptive enough to understand that he
has not ultimately relieved God of His responsibility although he has significantly shifted the grounds of inquiry.
The question is now one of the appropriateness of the
creation of man given the perfection of God. And there is
another question — whether the Jew after Auschwitz can
still bear witness to the presence of God:

> We have tried to show what is implied in Judaism's faith in the
> God of history independently of our contemporary experience.
> The question is, of course, well-grounded: Can such faith still be
> maintained in the face of the destruction of European Jewry?[50]

What is required for an affirmative response is a leap of
faith if not an additional belief in the messianic future. As
Berkovits writes:

> Yet all this does not exonerate God for all the suffering of the
> innocent in history. God is responsible for having created a world
> in which man is free to make history. There must be a dimension
> beyond history in which all suffering finds its redemption through
> God. This is essential to the faith of a Jew. The Jew does not
> doubt God's presence, though he is unable to set limits to the

50. *Ibid.*, p. 128.

duration and intensity of his absence. This is no justification for the ways of providence, but its acceptance. It is not a willingness to forgive the unheard cries of millions, but a trust that in God the tragedy of man may find its transformation.[51]

Ultimately, Berkovits is forced to rely upon the expectation of a messianic future.

Michael Wyschogrod, the other orthodox theologian I have considered, is similarly forced to reassert faith in the ultimate triumph of justice and to proclaim that in the end God will redeem. Both Wyschogrod and Berkovits understand that belief is difficult and that the credibility of their faith is subject to serious questioning by those inside and outside the circle of faith. But in the end for both Wyschogrod and Berkovits faith emerges triumphant.

For others, however, there is no faith; trust in both God and man has been shattered. In *Faith after the Holocaust* Berkovits writes:

Even if no answers could be found, we would still be left with the only alternative with which Job too was left, i.e. of contending with God while trusting in Him, of questioning while believing, *inquiring with our minds yet knowing in our hearts*. And even as we search for the answer, praising Him as the Rabbis of old did: Who is like you, our God, mighty in silence.[52] (italics mine)

For Elie Wiesel the struggle of the survivor is not merely an inquiry with the mind while knowing in the heart but a shattering of that knowledge, that trust in God. Wiesel's God is not a God who gave man freedom in history but rather a God who promised deliverance and remained silent in the hour of Israel's greatest need, a God who made it impossible to believe in the promise of future deliverance. Wiesel's theodicy is a theodicy of the void. His God is a

51. *Ibid.*, p. 136.
52. *Ibid.*, p. 113.

God of silence. Wiesel's struggle is to live in the face of the void.

Both Berkovits and Wiesel want to see Israel as central to the human drama. Both wish to mystify Jewish existence, and both refuse to speak of the Jew in the demystified words of Rubenstein as "neither more nor less than any other man." For Berkovits the mystification of Jewish existence entails a restatement of the Talmudic doctrine of Israel that provides the justification and the moral right for human existence. Wiesel wishes to make the same affirmation, but the intensity of his own experience forces him to speak of Israel in radically different terms. In opposition to Berkovits, Wiesel realizes, as does Rubenstein, that the state of Israel is not merely a continuation of the previous history of the Jewish people or an extension of their ongoing relationship with God but a revolution. His agony is intensified by his desire to affirm both God and Israel, as Berkovits does. However, Wiesel is unable to do so; he is far too honest to affirm that which would deny his most basic experiences.

Wiesel's literary works describe the agony and the torture of the Nazis' victims, an agony that was rooted in their mixed motivations of love and hate, responsibility and indifference, selfishness and selflessness. In *Night* he writes with painful honesty of his love for his father, of his fear of betrayal, and of his lapse into betrayal. Wiesel's characters are complex and multidimensional. His depiction of the suffering of the victims provides a complete context in which to understand their behavior, their rise to moments of glory and their fall to the abyss of human degradation. Berkovits, on the other hand, seems determined to document only the moments of glory when individuals achieved the highest in ethical and compassionate behavior. He therefore runs the risk of transforming the concentration camp experience into a heroic one rather than one of deeply tragic proportions. One can deeply sympathize with Berkovits' desire to protect the good name of the victims, but his catalogue of heroism tends to destroy the human quality of the victims. By comparison, Wiesel writes that "Saints are those who die before the end of the story. The others, those who live out their destiny, no longer dare look at themselves in the mirror, afraid they may see their inner image."[53]

In summary, when Wiesel is contrasted with his fellow contemporary theologians, one senses the uniqueness of his position and the agony of his dilemma. Unlike Rubenstein, he cannot really break with the traditional mythic and symbolic system of Judaism. He cannot free himself from its claims and understand himself in a radically demystified way. The past is ever-present for Wiesel, and the categories of the past restrict his ability to confront the present in an entirely new perspective. Unlike Fackenheim, Wiesel cannot ignore the most radical impact of the Auschwitz experience; he cannot distinguish between the forms of God's presence. Wiesel's God cannot be a saving God or a demanding God. If anything, his God is the God of laughter. "In the beginning there was neither the Word, nor Love, but laughter, the roaring, eternal laughter whose echoes are more deceitful than the mirages of the desert."[54] If anything, Wiesel's God is a God of silence, not a silence of enduring and waiting or a silence born of God shackling his omnipotence in order to allow man to experience history but a silence of indifference. "The lack of hate between murderer and victim, perhaps this is God."[55] Unlike Ber-

---

53. Elie Wiesel, *The Accident*, p. 49.
54. *Ibid.*, p. 42.
55. Elie Wiesel, *Dawn*, p. 76.

kovits (whose affirmations Wiesel would like to share), Wiesel must question the meaning of Israel, the nature of Israel's experience with God, and the quality of Israel's mission to the world. "In the beginning, there was Auschwitz,"[56] not Sinai and not creation.

In dialogue with his fellow contemporary theologians, the nature of the void becomes all the more apparent. Unlike Rubenstein, Wiesel cannot transcend the void. Unlike Fackenheim, he cannot shrink back from its consequences nor can he reaffirm a meaningful trust in the future as Berkovits does. Wiesel is radical enough to question but not radical enough to transgress beyond the theodicy. He is therefore forced to reunderstand the theodicy in the face of the void.

56. Elie Wiesel, "Jewish Values in the Post-Holocaust Future," p. 58.

Chapter Eight

Wiesel's Theory of the Holocaust

OUR ATTENTION has thus far been confined to Wiesel's theological position with respect to God and Israel after the Holocaust. This chapter will concentrate on Wiesel's conception of the Holocaust itself in order to further elucidate his theological position, especially his notion of solidarity, and in order to foster a greater understanding of Wiesel's role as survivor and witness. Wiesel's position with respect to the Holocaust is contradictory and paradoxical, and this paradox is central to his theological position. On the one hand, throughout his essays Wiesel attempts to defend the mystery of the Holocaust from the encroachments of objective analysis. He is disturbed by the cold objectivity of Hannah Arendt's historical analysis and by the limits of Bruno Bettelheim's psychological explanation.[1] Above all,

1. In "The Guilt We Share" Wiesel writes:

Well-known psychiatrists have attempted to give some explanation in their books dealing with the psychology of the concentration camp .... But to attribute that acceptance [of Nazi bestiality] — as they do — to the disintegration of the personality, or to the rising up of the "death wish," or to something in Jewish tradition, can only be a partial explanation. The metaphysical *why* is still lacking. (*Legends of Our Time,* pp. 209–210)

Wiesel is disturbed by the sense of detachment from events, which he finds in the analyses of Arendt, Bettelheim, and perhaps Hilberg[2] and by what he senses to be their judgment of the victims. In response, Wiesel asserts the essential mystery of the Holocaust and the inability of modern people and contemporary analysis to grasp fully the nature of the events.

On the other hand, Wiesel's novels reveal the weakness, as well as the strength, of people under the strain of extraordinary conditions, and Wiesel's tone is often highly critical. In fact, Bettelheim could point to Wiesel's novels, and most particularly to his memoir *Night,* to substantiate some of his own claims. In reality Wiesel's defense of the mystery of the Holocaust is but another confession of the void. Wiesel's assertion of the mystery preserves for the reader the holiness of the victims precisely at the point that Wiesel's writings reveal the compromises that were made. Wiesel's differences with Arendt and Bettelheim closely resemble his differences with Rubenstein; namely, that like many in the American Jewish community, Wiesel is uncomfortable with the use of analytic language and the abandonment of the mythic, symbolic system of traditional Judaism. Wiesel is troubled by the use of language that does not preserve the complexity of the original experience and that ignores its nuances and ambiguities. Furthermore, Wiesel

---

Since Bettelheim mentions the death instinct in his writings on the Holocaust (Bruno Bettelheim, *The Informed Heart* [New York: The Free Press, 1960], pp. 249–251) and since he is strongly criticized on this account (Alexander Donat, *Jewish Resistance* [New York: Warsaw Ghetto Resistance Organization, 1964]), it is safe to conclude that Wiesel had Bettelheim in mind when he wrote these words. My argument with respect to Wiesel's attack on Arendt will be presented below.

2. Wiesel's reference to "something in Jewish tradition" in the quote above may be a reference to Raul Hilberg's first chapter in *The Destruction of European Jewry* (Chicago: Quadrangle Books, 1961).

sees the collapse of one world view and chronicles its demise while he feels acute discomfort when others, who share his perceptions but do not openly manifest his pain, confront him with the reality they both perceive. Finally, some speculative reasons will be offered as to why Wiesel's position finds a responsive audience in the American Jew.

The Holocaust in Wiesel's Novels and Memoir and Bruno Bettelheim's Theory of the Holocaust: *The Informed Heart* and the Pained Soul

Bruno Bettelheim has been unrelenting in his critique of the "business as usual" attitude of the Jewish community during the Holocaust.[3] His choice of the Frank family as the perfect example of this attitude was bound to endear him to no one though it intensified the impact of his analysis. Bettelheim argues that the Jewish community failed to heed all of the warnings of impending doom and hence did not effectively mitigate their fate. Bettelheim criticized the Frank family for not separating in order to make their capture more difficult, for not making adequate escape provisions in their hideout, and for not pursuing the type of survival education that would have been so necessary had any member of the family escaped incarceration. Bettelheim furthermore argues that contemporary humanity has continuously refused to deal with the reality of the camps, for that reality would seriously damage their narcissistic pride in the accomplishments of modern civilization.[4] Jews cannot afford to delude themselves in this way for they have tragically experienced the peril of denial. As to the reasons why Jews did not revolt while in the camps, Bettelheim argues that they were trapped by their intense

3. *The Informed Heart*, pp. 246–249.
4. *Ibid.*, p. 247.

emotions. In order to effectively control the rage they felt toward the Nazis, the Jews exaggerated the Nazi threat to the point where it immobilized them. They were caught in a web of repression that was partly of their own making.[5]

Bettelheim has been severely criticized for his insensitivity to the agony of the Jews and for his emphasis on survival at any price.[6] However, Wiesel has not been criticized for his blatant expression of similar Jewish misperceptions and inaction. Bettelheim and Wiesel share similar perceptions though they speak from different perspectives. Bettelheim expresses his views in analytic language, which maintains a sense of objective distance[7] (and, at least for his critics, the posture of judgment), while Wiesel speaks in the first person and recreates the experience in rich subjectivity.

Elie Wiesel has claimed that he has written directly of

---

5. *Ibid.*, pp. 218–220.

6. Alexander Donat, *Jewish Resistance,* p. 57. It is ironic that in Bruno Bettelheim's recent essay in the *New Yorker* entitled "On Surviving" he bitterly denounces the Wertmuller movie *Seven Beauties* for its emphasis on survival at all costs. He is extremely frightened that our recent disappointment in the free world may lead to a fascination with totalitarianism and that this fascination could easily lead to active acceptance. He is angry at Wertmuller's use of farce and comedy for it seems to neutralize evil and to make a sham of human dignity. So much for Bettelheim's commitment to survival at any price. Bruno Bettelheim, "Surviving" in the *New Yorker* (August 2, 1976) pp. 31–52.

7. Bettelheim's passionate concern with humanity and with the moral issues raised by the Holocaust are easily seen in the *New Yorker* review essay. He writes:

> Her film (Wertmuller's) deals with the most important problems of our time, of all times; survival; good and evil; and man's attitude toward a life in which good and evil co-exist, when religion no longer offers guidance for dealing with this duality. The late Hannah Arendt . . . stressed the utter banality of evil. I agree with her thesis. But what must concern us primarily is that evil is evil . . . . (p. 33)

the Holocaust only in *Night*,[8] and it is in this memoir that Wiesel expresses his greatest impatience with the "business as usual" attitude that dominated his community. Wiesel wrote that in the spring of 1944 "people were interested in everything — in strategy, in diplomacy, in politics, in Zionism — but not in their own fate."[9] In his description of Sighet, he commented that even after the Nazis had arrived and the verdict had been pronounced, "the Jews of Sighet continued to smile."[10] Wiesel's imagery reflects his impatience with the skepticism with which all warnings were greeted. In *Night* the character who warns the others is Moshe the beadle.[11] In an "Evening Guest" Elijah brings evil tidings of doom rather than good tidings of the coming Messiah.[12] The messages are never heeded. Wiesel, like Bettelheim, is critical of the Jewish community's failure to confront reality and act accordingly.

Just as Bettelheim points to Anne Frank's education as an example of dysfunctional denial, Wiesel portrays characters whose education is similarly inappropriate to their situation. Both Eliezer in *Night* and Michael in *The Town Beyond the Wall*[13] are not trained to confront their situation. Eliezer was trained for eternity as history abruptly intruded into his life. Michael was saved from the madness of the mystical orchard only to enter the madness of the camps. Only Gavriel-Gregor in *The Gates of the Forest* confronted the reality of extermination, and he joins the

8. Elie Wiesel, "Talking and Writing and Keeping Silent," in Franklin H. Littell and Hubert Locke, eds., *The German Church Struggle and the Holocaust* (Detroit: Wayne State University Press, 1973), p. 270.

9. *Night*, p. 17.

10. *Ibid.*, p. 19.

11. *Ibid.*, pp. 12–17.

12. *Legends of Our Time*, pp. 43–51.

13. See chapter 1 of this work.

partisans in the forest. He survives through a combination of luck and audacity and through his initial refusal to delude himself.

The degree of self-delusion is even a shock to the inmates who can no longer accept the blindness of the outside world. In *Night* Wiesel describes the impatience with which the new arrivals at Auschwitz were greeted.[14] The inmates cannot believe that the world does not yet know and that people can still be arriving complacently for their own cremation. Wiesel continues to be critical of the Jews' repression of their fate. He described his family's decision not to uproot themselves and emigrate to Palestine and then immediately described the observance of Passover, which commemorates the Israelites' departure from Egypt in the middle of the night without sufficient time for their bread to rise. Just prior to the description of the Passover seder, Shlomo Wiesel comments:

"I'm too old, my son . . . I'm too old to start a new life. I'm too old to start from scratch again . . ."[15]

Ironically, Shlomo Wiesel renounces the possibility of a new life just as he celebrates the festival of spring. On the seventh day of Passover, Jews commemorate the saving at the Red Sea, and the "Song of the Sea"[16] is chanted in the synagogue. According to Wiesel's description in *Night,* it was precisely on the seventh day that the Jewish leaders of Sighet were arrested. The remembrance of God's saving presence and the faith that God will continue to save His people falsely consoled the people and contributed to their illusions. The race toward death had begun, yet Wiesel observed:

14. *Night,* pp. 40–41.
15. *Ibid.,* p. 18.
16. *Exodus* XV: 1–19.

The general opinion was that we were going to remain in the ghetto until the end of the war, until the arrival of the Red Army. Then everything would be as before. *It was neither German nor Jew who ruled the ghetto – it was illusion.*[17] (italics mine)

Foremost among the illusions was the illusion of time.

Throughout Wiesel's novels and short stories a character continually reappears who has been to the camps and seen their reality and returns to the world of the living only to be frustrated by the victims for various other reasons. For example, the young arrivals at the camps wish to revolt, yet their elders reply, "You must never lose faith, even when the sword hangs over your head. That's the teaching of our sages."[18] Wiesel's tone here emphasizes the delusionary and debilitating nature of their faith.

Lucy Dawidowicz in *The War Against the Jews* approaches Jewish behavior during the Holocaust from the perspective of Jewish sources.[19] She spoke of the importance of Jewish tradition, which emphasized the justice and goodness of what happened and taught that all must be accepted as good from God. The Jews saw themselves as co-workers with God and hence they responded with activity to impending danger, thus developing the virtues "of self-discipline, prudence, moderation, forgoing present gratification for eventual benefit."[20] Dawidowicz stresses the way Jews circumvented discrimination and deflected persecution. Jewish policy had a double thrust. Internal Jewish policy was aimed at bolstering morale, outwardly

17. *Night*, p. 21.
18. *Ibid.*, p. 41.
19. By comparison, Raul Hilberg's failure to use Jewish sources is considered by many to be the major flaw in an otherwise invaluable work. I do not concur with these judgments of Hilberg. As time goes on I increasingly appreciate his magisterial work.
20. *The War Against the Jews* (New York: Holt, Rinehart, Winston, and The Jewish Publication Society, 1975), p. 343.

alleviating hardship, and nullifying persecution.[21] Although
Dawidowicz does not deal with the concentration camp
situation except for the briefest references, the policies of
the Jewish organizations are accurately and thoroughly
described by her. The early Wiesel, the author of *Night*,
felt that the bolstering of morale was a costly self-deception
for the Jews while Bettelheim could easily see in
Dawidowicz's descriptive documentation the persistence of
a business-as-usual attitude among the Jews. As
Dawidowicz clearly shows, the nomos of the community
re-established itself again quite quickly despite the anomic
situation.

Wiesel does not shrink from exposing negative aspects
of the victims' behavior, refusing to unequivocally heroize
the victims. In *Night* Wiesel describes the moments of
anomie in which each man battled on his own for survival.
The moments were the ones in which fathers betrayed sons
and sons fathers. Rabbi Eliahou's son ran away[22] from his
father, and Eliezer resented the burden of his father's presence and briefly abandoned him.[23] Wiesel coninually describes the price paid for survival both in terms of what has
been called survivors' guilt and in terms of the knowledge
of one's limited humanity. Wiesel recounts his reaction to
the death of his father:

I did not weep, and it pained me that I could not weep. But I had
no more tears. And, in the depths of my being, in the recesses of
my weakened conscience, could I have searched it, I might perhaps have found something like — free at last.[24]

Eliezer was freed of the burden of his father, but he was
also bereft of his father's love. During the next months he

21. *Ibid.*, p. 345.
22. *Ibid.*, pp. 102–104.
23. *Ibid.*, pp. 116–124.
24. *Ibid.*, p. 124.

lived as if in a haze without reason and without hope, consumed by his own guilt and the memory of betrayal. The tale of *Night* is a tale of fratricide and patricide as well as a tale of filial love and devotion. The moments of betrayal predominate, but there are also moments of triumph, moments when the young boy chooses death over betrayal[25] or when the condemned man proclaims "Long live liberty! A curse on Germany! A curse . . ."[26] The complexity of the picture that Wiesel presents forces the reader to confront nuances of meaning, meaning that Wiesel fears might be lost in abstractions.

The Holocaust in the Essays of Elie Wiesel

While Wiesel's novels portray Jewish behavior in all its complexity without distorting the moments of human collapse or of human triumph, his essays present Jewish behavior in a rather different light. In fairness to Wiesel, it must be stated that his essays are written in response (and often in polemic response) to portrayals of Jewish behavior that Wiesel perceives as insensitive to the anguish of the human situation. In his essays Wiesel is usually quite defensive about the victims' behavior and is highly critical toward the behavior of the world, including world Jewry.

Wiesel's defensive posture often sounds apologetic. The reader is informed that the Jews did not rebel "to punish us, to prepare a vengeance for us for later."[27] While in his memoir *Night* Wiesel depicts the affirmations of faith by the elders in response to the young men's cries for revolt, in his essays Wiesel presents a different response. The young men continue to demand revolt:

25. *Ibid.*, p. 74–76.
26. *Ibid.*, p. 74.
27. *Legends of Our Time*, p. 233.

Even if you are right . . . even if what you say is true, that doesn't change the situation. Let us prove our courage and our dignity, let us show these murderers and the world that Jews know how to die like free men, not like hunched-up invalids.[28]

However, the elder's reply no longer speaks of faith but of condemnation of all mankind. One old man replied: "As a lesson, I like that . . . But they don't deserve it."[29] In addition, even Sighet's unpreparedness and unresponsiveness to the danger at hand is cast in a new light in Wiesel's essays. Wiesel argues that the Jews of Sighet listened to the radio and heard foreign broadcasts but that none of these broadcasts warned them of their fate.[30] Their ignorance is no longer treated as a failure to confront reality but as proof of the world's guilt.

I wish to emphasize the fact that I write of Wiesel's defensiveness without any pejorative implication. The world's neglect of the Jew's fate and the Jew's resistance to facing that fate are both parts of the historical reality. However, in his essays Wiesel chooses to concentrate on the world's responsibility. There is, however, one major danger in Wiesel's defensiveness and that is that it may deprecate some of the valuable insights into Jewish behavior and the human condition that are now available in analytic writings.

One of the major functions of Wiesel's treatment of the Holocaust presented in his essays, as opposed to his memoir and novels, is the effective engenderment of guilt. In his final two essays of *Legends of Our Time,* "The Guilt We Share" and "A Plea for the Dead," Wiesel explores the phenomena of guilt. In "The Guilt We Share" Wiesel uses guilt to spur Jewish action, to explain Jewish behavior, and to undermine the moral credibility of the Western world.

28. *Ibid.,* p. 228.
29. *Ibid.*
30. *Ibid.,* p. 229.

No one emerges from the Holocaust without a stain of guilt. The Allies are castigated for their refusal to bomb the camps, America is rebuked for its failure to intervene, neutral countries are criticized for their neutrality, and world Jewry is faulted for its relative indifference and inaction. Wiesel's expectations for world Jewry are enormous, and although he has a genuine right to feel betrayed, his hopes are inflated by the mythic power he attributes to solidarity. He writes:

The American Jewish community never made adequate use of its political and financial powers; *certainly it did not move heaven and earth, as it should have.*[31] (italics mine)

A belief in the mystic powers of solidarity should not obscure the perception of class differences and conflicting loyalties which contributed to Jewish inaction. However, Wiesel may sense that the universalization of Jewish guilt can be a successful strategy for overcoming these differences in cases that require concerted Jewish efforts, such as the state of Israel and Soviet Jewry.

Wiesel also uses guilt in another context as an explanation for Jewish compliance. Wiesel claims that in the camps the Jews did not revolt because they were consumed by their own guilt as survivors. The victims realized that to be alive was to be guilty, for to be alive meant that you were "the cause, perhaps the condition, of someone else's death."[32] To live was to be compromised, and to revolt would have meant to betrayal of the dead.

To die struggling would have meant a betrayal of those who had gone to their death submissive and silent. The only way was to follow in their footsteps, die their kind of death — only then could the living make their peace with those who had already gone.[33]

31. *Legends of Our Time*, p. 205.
32. *Ibid.*, p. 210.
33. *Ibid.*, p. 212.

Fidelity to the dead meant following in their footsteps. Throughout his essay Wiesel uses guilt to defend the victims, to castigate the bystanders, and to deny everyone the right to judge.

As has been previously mentioned, Wiesel is angered by the tones of self-assurance that permeate objective considerations of the Holocaust. He is concerned that the Jews may be held responsible for their own deaths and that the responsibility of the Nazis will thus be diminished. He is also furious at the imposition of degrading motives to the actions of the dead.

What, then, is Wiesel's plea for the dead? On the one hand, Wiesel argues for silence. He fears that reflection after the experience may distort or diminish the experience. Yet all of his work and his commitment to the task of witness reflects his own inability to remain silent, so that silence is emphatically not the final response. Wiesel suggests that one must assume a specific attitude toward the Holocaust and that within the framework of that attitude one is permitted to ask certain questions. He seems to compare the Holocaust to the Talmudic description of *Pardes,* the mystical orchard where the punishment of the innocent is contemplated. One must not enter the orchard too easily for one runs the risk of madness, loss of innocence, and death, yet only by entering the orchard and identifying with the pain of the victims does one earn the right to question. Prior to the identification with the victims, silence is demanded. Otherwise, the memory of the dead and the mystery of the experience might be eclipsed. Wiesel recounts a conversation he held with one of the judges at the Eichmann trial. He asked the judge if he understood the Holocaust, and the judge replied:

"No, not at all. . . . There is in all this a portion which will always remain a mystery: a kind of forbidden zone, inaccessible to reason. . . . Who knows, perhaps that's the gift which God, in a moment of grace, gave to man: it prevents him from understanding everything, thus saving him from madness, or from suicide."[34]

For Wiesel the Holocaust is a mystery that should be protected from the process of demystification. The analytic writings of the historian, the critical tone that assimilates and evaluates facts, threaten to destroy the mystery and rob it of its power. In a sense, the historian and the social scientist go beyond the void by participating in a conceptual universe which, though not necessarily insensitive to the pain of lost meaning, possesses a vocabulary far removed from the domain of metaphysics and ontology and hence from the void that Wiesel so intensely describes.

For Wiesel "The revolt of the believer is not that of the renegade."[35] He asks:

Can you compare . . . the tragedy of the believer to that of the non-believer? The real tragedy, the real drama, is the drama of the believer.[36]

The real dimensions upon which Wiesel demands a response are the metaphysical and the ontological dimensions. The medium that best captures the dimensions of pain and ambiguity is the tale with its open-ended reality. The reason Wiesel rejects all answers is because, on the metaphysical and ontological levels, his experience is profoundly that of the void. The void is best expressed by the question that remains a question in quest of an answer.

One of Wiesel's more recent essays on the Holocaust shows yet another dimension of his lowering of expectation and also indicates his own solidarity with the survivors as

34. *Ibid.*, p. 223.
35. *Souls on Fire*, p. 111.
36. Elie Wiesel, "Talking and Writing and Keeping Silent," p. 274.

he once felt his place was with the dead. While his earlier essay was entitled "A Plea for the Dead," his more recent essay was entitled "A Plea for the Survivors." He moved to the world of the living who, like Isaac, had experienced death and returned. (Wiesel's plea, ironically, is quoted approvingly by Bettelheim in his article on surviving.) Wiesel bemoans the cheapening of the Holocaust and the loss of humility: "As the subject becomes popularized, so it ceased to be sacrosanct or rather was stripped of its mystery. People lost their awe."[37] Like Bettelheim, Wiesel sees himself in a community of people who have survived and who are increasingly disturbed by the misuse of their experience, by their own inability to fully explain their experience, and by a contemporary fascination with the killers. Both Wiesel and Bettelheim realize that survivors won't be around much longer, and both fear that the survivor is the only one who knows.

Ontology and History: Wiesel and Arendt

Although Wiesel appears to resent Hannah Arendt's work on the Holocaust, a comparison between Arendt's approach and Wiesel's will clarify the differences between Wiesel's metaphysical and ontological concern as opposed to a more sociological orientation. Furthermore, some specific criticisms that Wiesel makes in his "Plea for the Dead" are weak, and their weakness exposes the limitations of Wiesel as a systematic thinker just as previous discussion has shown his power as a writer.

It seems clear that Wiesel's "Plea for the Dead" is written in response to Hannah Arendt's *Echmann in Jerusalem*. The juxtaposition of Wiesel's tirade against judgment and Wiesel's insistence on an attitude of shared

37. Elie Wiesel, "A Plea for the Survivors," p. 2.

pain with the repeated reference to Eichmann, *Judenrat,* and awards for good and bad conduct allows no other possible conclusion, for in every significant detail the position that Wiesel criticizes is the position that Hannah Arendt is said to hold by her major Jewish critics.[38] It is clear that for many, including Gershom Scholem, the manner in which Arendt said her piece was as offensive, if not more offensive, than what she said.

Wiesel's first criticism against many analytic studies of the Holocaust and presumably against Arendt involves the relationship between Nazi responsibility and Jewish behavior. Wiesel writes that:

Beyond the diversity of all theories, the self-assurance of which cannot but arouse anger, all unanimously conclude that the victims by participating in the executioner's game, in varying degrees shared responsibility.[39]

This charge, which is repeated by Alexander Donat in his criticism of Arendt,[40] seems misplaced when directed at Arendt.

38. See Ernst Simon, "A Textual Examination," and Alexander Donat, "An Empirical Examination," in "Revisionist History of the Jewish Catastrophe: Two Examinations of Hannah Arendt," in *Judaism,* Vol. XII, No. 4 (Fall 1963), pp. 388–435. Similarly, a strongly negative evaluation of Professor Arendt's work is to be found in Norman Podhoretz, "Hannah Arendt on Eichmann: A Study in the Perversity of Brilliance," in *Commentary,* Vol. XXXVI, No. 9 (September 1963). The most positive review of Arendt's work is Bruno Bettelheim's "Eichmann: The System, The Victims," in *The New Republic,* Vol. 148, No. 24 (June 15, 1963), pp. 23–33.

39. *Legends of Our Time,* p. 219.

40. See note 38. Arendt makes her point on the complicity of leadership as part of a much larger theory of totalitarian domination and it should not be considered in isolation from her entire theory. Ironically, it was Arendt's work that set the tone for future Holocaust research and led to Isaiah Trunk's *Judenrat* (New York: The Macmillan Co., 1972) and Raul Hilberg's forthcoming translation and commentary on the diary of Adam Cheriakow, the leader of the Warsaw Judenrat.

Arendt goes to great lengths to underscore the persistent differences between the conceptual universes of the Germans and that of the rest of the world. In one of the most poignant dialogues recounted in *Eichmann in Jerusalem,* Professor Arendt writes:

Servatius declared the accused innocent of charges bearing on his responsibility for "the collection of skeletons, sterilizations, killings by gas, and *similar medical matters,*" whereupon Judge Halevi interrupted him: "Dr. Servatius, I assume you made a slip of the tongue when you said that killing by gas was a medical matter." To which Servatius replied: "It was indeed a medical matter, since it was prepared by physicians; it was *a matter of killing and killing, too, is a medical matter.*"[41]

Servatius later repeated this remark. Arendt suggests that perhaps Servatius wanted to

Make absolutely sure that the judges in Jerusalem would not forget how Germans — ordinary Germans, not former members of the SS or even the Nazi party — even today can regard an act that in other countries is called murder.[42]

Professor Arendt in no way wishes to exonerate the Germans and in no way equates German responsibility with Jewish responsibility.

Wiesel criticizes numerous theoreticians for indicating what he calls a "shared responsibility"; however, the responsibility of the perpetrators is not in the same category as the response of the victims. Inadequate self-defense does not lessen the guilt of the murderer. One thinks of the feminist's insistence that whatever the behavior of the rape victim, it is the rapist who must be held responsible. When

41. Hannah Arendt, *Eichmann in Jerusalem* (New York: Viking Press, 1963), p. 69.
42. *Ibid.,* p. 69.

the feminists advocate preventative behavior on the part of the potential victim to minimize the possibility of rape, they in no way exonerate the rapist. Similarly, Arendt's claims as to the victim's behavior, as well as that of the perpetrators, is for the purpose of understanding and prevention rather than to minimize Nazi responsibility.

Wiesel's insistence upon the mystery of the Holocaust and upon the continuity between traditional anti-Semitism and the Holocaust runs the risk of mitigating against the most basic and unique aspect of Arendt's and Hilberg's understanding of the Holocaust, namely their refusal to view the extermination of the Jews as a direct continuation of medieval and modern anti-Semitism. Arendt argues that to fully understand the concentration camps, the camps must not be seen exclusively in their Jewish context, i.e. as an unrestrained outbreak of anti-Semitism, but also as an extension onto the domestic front of the policies of imperialism which were the end result of the unrestrained expansionary drive of industrial capitalism. The Jews became the chosen victims not only because of the traditions of anti-Semitism but also because they were economically superfluous to Germany and possessed visible power without wealth.[43] One logical method of eliminating a superfluous population (and the reader must bear in mind that logical is not equivalent to moral or desirable) is by extermination. Arendt follows Raul Hilberg and argues that the Jewish institutions failed to perceive correctly their own situation and hence the responses that they had practiced for two millenia in dealing with anti-Semitism were hopelessly inappropriate to their unprecedented situation.[44]

43. See Hannah Arendt, *The Origins of Totalitarianism* (Cleveland: The World Publishing Company, 1951), most specifically chapter 1.
44. *The Destruction of European Jewry,* Hilberg writes:

Both perpetrators and victims drew upon their age-old experience in

They did not understand the inherent lawlessness of the
Nazi regime and the fact that the Nazis were operating
without any of the traditional moral, social, political, and
economic constraints that had limited the scope of previous
anti-Semitic outbreaks.[45]

Arendt's treatment of Eichmann as a bureaucrat with
the basic skills of organization and negotiation is totally
consistent with her understanding of the Holocaust. She
seeks to analyze the man. Her understanding of Eichmann
is often in direct conflict with the role ascribed to him by the
prosecutor for the state of Israel[46] and with the role ascribed to him by Wiesel.[47] She describes Eichmann not as a
demonic monster but as a bureaucratic functionary who
would commit his full allegiance to any system that could
reward his talents and arouse his enthusiasm.[48] This bureaucratic Eichmann is in a way far more dangerous than
the demonic monster because of his prevalence in a modern

---

dealing with each other. The Germans did it with success. The Jews
did it with disaster. (p. 17)

See also *Eichmann in Jerusalem,* pp. 117 ff.

45. For an updating of the dangers described by both Hilberg and
Arendt, see Richard L. Rubenstein's *The Cunning of History* (New
York: Harper and Row, 1976). Here too Rubenstein strives to describe
the Holocaust in a radically demystified fashion while Wiesel is seeking
to protect the mystery.

46. Gideon Hausner, *Justice in Jerusalem* (New York: Harper and
Row, 1965).

47. In the essay "The Guilt We Share," Wiesel describes Eichmann
as a liar determined to save his own neck, and thus he agrees with both
the prosecution and the judges. However, he concedes that Eichmann
may not have been a major actor in the German drama, and thus he
concurs on this fundamental point with Arendt.

There are any number of difficulties which stem from Wiesel's refusal to attack his adversaries by name and to enter into dialogue rather
than standing aloof and remaining 'above' the dialogues. I find his course
of action somewhat unwise.

48. *Eichmann in Jerusalem,* pp. 21–36.

technological society and because of his passionless amorality which can operate so methodically.

David Bakan has suggested that the two descriptions of Eichmann, the bureaucrat and the demon, are far closer to each other than one would ordinarily expect. He minimizes the area of disagreement:

The externalization of necessity is often buttressed by both an ultra-mythicism and an ultra-realism. Both were present, for example, in the great holocaust of Nazism with the revival of German historical myths, on the one hand, and the complete banality — to borrow Hannah Arendt's term for it — and excessive realism of orderliness, obedience, bureaucracy, files, schedules, supplies, etc., of Eichmann, on the other. Although ultra-mythicism and ultra-realism appear to be poles apart, they are identical in that in both there is the externalization of necessity. There is only a superficial contrast between them.[49]

In both the demonic and the bureaucratic characterizations, Eichmann eludes the full measure of personal responsibility, in the one case because his extraordinary evil places him beyond the realm of ordinary humanity and in the other case because he is the victim and the creation of a depersonalized, technological system.

Wiesel's insistence on the mystery of the Holocaust is in conflict with Arendt's struggle for comprehension. Arendt writes:

Comprehension does not mean denying the outrageous, deducing the unprecedented from precedents, or explaining phenomena by such analogies and generalities that the impact of reality and the shock of experience are no longer felt . . . Comprehension, in short, means the unpremeditated, attentive, facing up to and resisting of reality — whatever it may be.[50]

49. David Bakan, *Disease, Pain, and Sacrifice* (Chicago: The University of Chicago Press, 1968), p. 117.
50. *The Origins of Totalitarianism*, p. viii.

For Arendt, the unpleasant reality that we must face is external: social, economic, psychological, political, historical, and moral. For Wiesel the reality that must be confronted, and the reality upon which we risk our souls in confrontation, is ontological. There is no reason why the one reality need preclude the other, though Wiesel seems to feel that the understanding of the psycho-social situation without asking the ontological question is limited and distorts reality. It is appropriate to suggest that the opposite is also the case and that Wiesel's insistence on the mystery threatens to distort parts of reality that must be confronted.

Wiesel's Defense of Mystery and the Roots of His Attraction to American Jewry: A Speculative Theory

The question must be asked as to why Wiesel's writings, with respect to the mystery of the Holocaust, find a responsive audience in American Jewry while the demystified writings of Arendt qua historian, of Rubenstein qua theologian, and of Bettelheim qua psychoanalyst meet with such hostility? Elsewhere it has been suggested that the problem was related to Wiesel's reaffirmation of the viability of the Jewish symbolic system and to the other writers' detachment from that conceptual system. In this section I would like to offer the broad outlines of a psychoanalytic understanding of the mystery of the Holocaust. The leadership of American Jewry has responded quite hostilely to the three major attempts to demystify the history of the Holocaust and the one theological attempt that spoke in radically demystified terms.[51] Only in the deep groundswell of support for the state of Israel has the Jewish community really confronted and responded to the Holocaust. The American

51. See chapter 7.

Jewish community's refusal to face the Holocaust in a de-mystified way may have deep psychological roots.

From Wiesel's writings and from the writings of other authors, we learn of the patricidal and infanticidal impulses that were sometimes expressed in the behavior of the victims. It is no accident that the victims were burned, offered up, as it were, as sacrifices on an altar. The emphasis on the innocence of the victims seems to reflect the sacrificial requirement that the offering be without blemish. The innocence of the children particularly emphasizes the un-blemished quality of the offering. Several authors have also referred to the victims as messiahs, atoning sacrifices offered up on an altar. Though these references are often unintentional, their unconscious significance is important.

The contradictory attitudes toward the victims and the survivors must also be considered. These attitudes reflect a profound ambivalence and welcome a sense of mystery. Eliezer Berkovits spoke of the 'holiness of the victims' and the unique authority of the survivors. His writings are not alone in their insistence upon an attitude of veneration and holiness with respect to the victims and survivors. Yet, on the other hand, Wiesel (and not only Wiesel) stresses the compromised behavior of the inmates in the camps, that all who have emerged are defiled. The unspeakable question that is never asked of the survivor, "How did you survive?" and the uncomfortableness one feels in his presence may relate as much to personal compromise as it does to holiness.

This sense of the holiness of the victims and the mystery of the Holocaust may be rooted in what psychoanalysis has termed the primal crime. Whether one understands the primal crime in the Freudian sense of patricide or in the Bakanian sense of infanticide is unimportant. The anger and the competition that are present in the institution of the family as well as the love and concern evident in that web of relationships leaves us with an enormous sense of ambivalence. Acting out either of these tendencies without restraint is considered the most sinful of human acts. Any memory of such sinful acts tends to be repressed and resurfaces in the extreme opposite of veneration and sacredness, for once the hostility is expressed, the love and the concern, which are the other side of our ambivalent feelings, are able to fully express themselves. One need not argue that the victims and the survivors were fratricidal or infanticidal. Rather, one may speculate that our fears of our own actions under such circumstances and our fright as to which series of emotions would become dominant within us leads us to overestimate the behavior of the victims and to shroud the event in mystery. We are trapped by our own ambivalence and perhaps by the communal memory of some primal crime (taken in a serious, though non-literal sense).

If this be the case, then Wiesel, an author whose fundamental perspective on the Holocaust mirrors this ambivalence of sinfulness and holiness, mystery and the quest for explanation, finds an audience of kindred souls in American Jews. Wiesel presents all sides of the questions raised by the Holocaust. He also stands at the brink with respect to God. He loves Him and hates Him, he fears Him and yet tries to live without Him. Common to his treatment of God, Israel, and the Holocaust is this standing on the brink. Wiesel is torn by ambivalence as he confronts the void.

Bibliography

Abramowitz, Molly. *Elie Wiesel: An Annotated Bibliography.* Metuchen, N. J.: The Scarecrow Press, 1974.

Alter, Robert. *After the Tradition: Essays on Modern Jewish Writing.* New York: E.P. Dutton & Co., 1969.

Arendt, Hannah. *Eichmann in Jerusalem.* New York: Viking Press, 1963.

―――. *The Origins of Totalitarianism.* Cleveland: The World Publishing Company, 1951.

Bakan, David. *Disease, Pain, and Sacrifice.* Chicago: The University of Chicago Press, 1968.

―――. *Sigmund Freud and the Jewish Mystical Tradition.* New York: Schocken Books, 1958.

―――. *The Duality of Human Existence.* Boston: Beacon Press, 1966.

Bernstein, Richard J. *Praxis and Action.* Philadelphia: The University of Pennsylvania Press, 1971.

Berger, Peter. *The Sacred Canopy: Elements of a Sociological Theory of Religion.* Garden City: Doubleday & Co., Inc., 1967.

Berger, Peter, and Luckmann, Thomas. *The Social Construction of Reality: A Treatise in the Sociology of Reality.* Garden City: Doubleday & Co., Inc., 1966.

Berkovits, Eliezer. *Faith after the Holocaust.* New York: Ktav, 1973.

Bettelheim, Bruno. "Eichmann: The System, The Victims." *The New Republic*, Vol. 148, No. 24, June 15, 1963.

――――. "Individual and Mass Behavior in Extreme Situations." *Journal of Abnormal and Social Psychology*, Vol. 38, 1943.

――――. "Surviving." *New Yorker*, August 2, 1976.

――――. "The Dynamism of Anti-Semitism in Gentile and Jew." *Journal of Abnormal and Social Psychology*, Vol. 42, No. 2, 1942.

――――. *The Informed Heart*. Chicago: The Free Press, 1960.

Borowitz, Eugene. "Covenant Theology — Another Look." *World View*, Vol. 16, No. 3, March 1973.

Buber, Martin. *Eclipse of God*. New York: Harper and Row, 1952.

――――. *Tales of Rabbi Nachman*. New York: Horizon Press, Inc., 1956.

――――. *Tales of the Hasidim*. New York: Schocken Books, 1947.

――――. *The Legends of the Baal Shem*. New York: Harper and Row, 1955.

Brigg, Emil, and Tabori, Paul. *Stand Up and Fight*. London: George Harrap & Co. Ltd., 1972.

Camus, Albert. *The Rebel*. New York: Vintage Books, 1956.

Cargas, Harry James. *Harry James Cargas in Conversation with Elie Wiesel*. Paramus: Paulist Press, 1976.

Cleaver, Eldridge. *Soul on Ice*. New York: Dell Publishing Co., 1968.

Cohen, Arthur, ed. *Arguments and Doctrines: A Reader of Jewish Thinking in the Aftermath of the Holocaust*. New York: Harper & Row, 1970.

――――. "Franz Rosenzweig's *The Star of Redemption:* An Inquiry into Its Psychological Origins." *Midstream*, Vol. XVIII, No. 2, February 1972.

――――. *In the Days of Simon Stern*. New York: Random House, 1973.

Cohn, Norman. *The Pursuit of the Millennium*. New York: Oxford University Press, 1960.

Cone, James. *Black Theology of Liberation*. Philadelphia: J.B. Lippincott Co., 1970.

Cunningham, Lawrence. "*Night* as Anti-Exodus." Unpublished article.

Cutler, D. R., ed. *The Religious Situation, 1968*. Boston: Beacon Press, 1969.

Cutler, D. R., and Richardson, Herbert W., eds. *Transcendence*. Boston: Beacon Press, 1969.

Davidowitz, Lucy, ed. *The Golden Tradition*. Boston: Beacon Press, 1967.

————. *The War against the Jews*. New York: Holt, Rinehart & Winston, 1975.

Des Pres, Terrence. *The Survivor: An Anatomy of Life in the Death Camps*. New York: Oxford University Press, 1976.

Donat, Alexander. *Jewish Resistance*. New York: Warsaw Ghetto Resistance Organization, 1964.

————. *The Holocaust Kingdom*. New York: Holt, Rinehart, and Winston, 1963.

————. "Revisionist History of Jewish Catastrophe: Two Examinations of Hannah Arendt." *Judaism*, Vol. 12, No. 4, Fall 1973.

Esh, Saul. "The Dignity of the Destroyed." *Judaism*, Vol. 15, No. 1, Winter 1966.

Ezrachi, Sidra. "The Holocaust in Literature." Ph.D. dissertation, Brandeis University, 1976.

Fackenheim, Emil. *Encounters Between Judaism and Modern Philosophy*. New York: Basic Books, Inc., 1973.

————. *God's Presence in History*. New York: New York University Press, 1969.

————. *Quest for Past and Future*. Boston: Beacon Press, 1968.

————. *The Religious Dimension in Hegel's Thought*. Bloomington: Indiana University Press, 1967.

————. *The Jewish Return into History: Reflections in the Age of Auschwitz and a New Jerusalem*. New York: Schocken Books, 1978.

Federn, Ernst. "The Terror as a System: The Concentration Camp," *Psychiatric Quarterly Supplements*, Vol. 22, 1948.

Fiske, Edward. "Elie Wiesel — Activist with a Mission." *New York Times*, January 31, 1973.

Fleischner, Eva, ed. *Auschwitz: Beginning of a New Era*. New York: Ktav Publishing House, 1977.

Frankl, Victor. *Man's Search for Meaning*. Boston: Beacon Press, 1963.

Freud, Sigmund. Trans. and ed. by James Strachey. *Beyond the Pleasure Principle.* New York: Bantam Books, Inc., 1959.
————. *The Ego and the Id.* New York: W.W. Norton and Co., Inc., 1960.
————. *Civilization and Its Discontents.* New York: W.W. Norton and Co., Inc., 1961.
————. Ed. by Katherine Jones. *Moses and Monotheism.* New York: Random House, 1955.
————. *Group Psychology and the Analysis of the Ego.* New York: Bantam Books, Inc., 1960.
————. *Totem and Taboo.* New York: W.W. Norton and Co., Inc., 1952.
Friedlander, Albert, ed. *Out of the Whirlwind: An Anthology of Holocaust Literature.* New York: Union of American Hebrew Congregations, 1968.
Friedman, Maurice. *To Deny Our Nothingness: Contemporary Images of Man.* New York: Delacorte Press, 1967.
Green, Arthur. *Rabbi Nachman of Bratzlav: A Critical Biography.* University: The University of Alabama Press, 1979.
Greenberg, Irving, and Rosenfeld, Alvin. *Confronting the Holocaust.* Bloomington: Indiana University Press, 1979.
Halpern, Irving. *Messengers from the Dead.* Philadelphia: Westminster Press, 1970.
Hausner, Gideon. *Justice in Jerusalem.* New York: Harper & Row, Inc., 1966.
Hegel, G. W. F. *Early Theological Writings.* Chicago: The University of Chicago Press, 1948.
Heimler, Eugene. *Concentration Camp.* New York: Vanguard Press, Inc., 1959.
Hertzberg, Arthur, ed. *The Zionist Idea.* Philadelphia: Jewish Publication Society, 1959.
Heschel, Abraham Joshua. *A Passion for Truth.* New York: Farrar, Straus, and Giroux, 1973.
————. *Israel: An Echo of Eternity.* New York: Farrar, Straus, and Giroux, 1969.
————. *The Earth Is the Lord's.* New York: Farrar, Straus, and Giroux, 1950.
Hilberg, Raul. *The Destruction of European Jewry.* Chicago: Quadrangle Books, 1961.

————. *Documents of Destruction*. Chicago: Quadrangle Books, 1971.

Indinopulos, Thomas. "The Holocaust in the Stories of Elie Wiesel." *Soundings,* Vol. 55, No. 2, Summer 1972.

Jacob, Louis. *Seeker of the Unity*. New York: Basic Books, 1966.

Kahane, Meir. *Never Again*. New York: Pyramid Books, 1972.

Kaplan, Chaim. *Scroll of Agony*. New York: The MacMillan Company, 1965.

Kaplan, Mordecai. *Judaism as a Civilization*. New York: The MacMillan Company, 1935.

————. *Judaism without Supernaturalism*. New York: Jewish Reconstructionist Foundation, Inc., 1958.

Ka-tzetnik 131633. *House of Dolls*. New York: Pyramid Books, 1960.

————. *Phoenix Over the Galilee*. New York: Harper & Row, 1969.

Kaufmann, Walter. *Nietzsche*. Princeton: Princeton University Press, 1950.

Keniston, Kenneth. *Young Radicals*. New York: Harcourt, Brace & World, Inc., 1968.

Kosinski, Jerzy. *The Painted Bird*. Boston: Houghton Mifflin Co., 1965.

Kruk, Herman. "Diary of the Vilna Ghetto." *YIVO Annual of Jewish Social Science,* Vol. VIII, 1965.

Langer, Lawrence. *The Holocaust and the Literary Imagination*. New Haven: Yale University Press, 1975.

Langer, Walter. *The Mind of Adolph Hitler*. New York: The New American Library, Inc., 1972.

Levin, Nora. *The Holocaust*. New York: Thomas Y. Crowell Co., 1968.

Lewinska, Pelagia. *Twenty Months at Auschwitz*. Trans. by Albert Teichner. Secaucus, N. J.: Lyle Stuart Publishers, Inc., 1968.

Lind, Jakov. *Counting My Steps*. Riverside, N. J.: Macmillan Publishing Co., 1969.

————. *Souls of Wood*. New York: Grove Press, Inc., 1964.

Littell, Franklin H., and Locke, Hubert, eds. *The German Church Struggle and the Holocaust*. Detroit: Wayne State University Press, 1973.

Marx, Karl, and Engels, Friedrich. *On Religion*. New York: Schocken Books, 1964.

Memmi, Albert. *The Liberation of the Jew*. New York: The Viking Press, 1973.

Midrash Rabbah. Trans. under the editorship of H. Freedman and Maurice Simon. 10 vols. London: Soncino Press, 1939.

Midrash Tanchuma. Ed. by S. Buber. Wilna: Romm, 1885.

Mintz, Jerome. *Legends of the Hasidim*. Chicago: The University of Chicago Press, 1968.

Mintz, Jerome, and Ben-Amos, Dan. *In Praise of the Baal Shem Tov*. Bloomington: Indiana University Press, 1970.

Morse, Arthur. *While Six Million Died*. New York: Random House, 1968.

Neusner, Jacob. *American Judaism*. Englewood Cliffs: Prentice-Hall, Inc., 1972.

————. *From Politics to Piety*. Englewood Cliffs: Prentice-Hall, Inc., 1973.

————. "The Implications of the Holocaust." *The Journal of Religion*, Vol. 53, No. 3, Summer 1973.

————. *There We Sat Down*. Nashville: Abingdon Press, 1972.

Nietzche, Friedrich. *The Genealogy of Morals*. New York: Random House, 1967.

Nissenson, Hugh. *In the Reign of Peace*. New York: Farrar, Straus, and Giroux, 1972.

Nyiszli, Miklos. *Auschwitz*. New York: Frederick Fell, Inc., 1960.

Oppenheimer, Rivka Schatz. *Hasidism as Mysticism*. Jerusalem: Judah Magnes Press, 1968.

Panken, Shirley. *The Joy of Suffering*. New York: Jason Aronson, Inc., 1973.

Pinkus, Oscar. *The House of Ashes*. Cleveland: The World Publishing Company, 1964.

Podhoretz, Norman. "Hannah Arendt on Eichmann: A Study in the Perversity of Brilliance." *Commentary*, Vol. XXXVI, No. 9, September 1963.

Reitlinger, Gerald. *The Final Solution*. South Brunswick: Thomas Yoseloff, 1953.

Ringelblum, Emmanuel. *Notes from the Warsaw Ghetto*. New York: McGraw-Hill Book Co., Inc., 1958.

Roiskes, David. *The Shtetl.* New York: Ktav Publishing House, 1975.

Rosenbaum, Irving. *The Holocaust and Halakhah.* New York: Ktav Publishing House, 1976.

Rosenzweig, Franz. *The Star of Redemption.* New York: Holt, Rinehart and Winston, 1970.

Roth, John. *A Consuming Fire.* Atlanta: J. B. Knox, forthcoming.

Rubenstein, Richard L. *After Auschwitz.* Indianapolis: The Bobbs-Merrill Company, Inc., 1968.

————. "God as Cosmic Sadist." *Christian Century,* Vol. 87, No. 30, July 29, 1970.

————. "Job and Auschwitz." *Union Seminary Quarterly Review,* Vol. XXV, No. 4, Summer 1970.

————. *Morality and Eros.* New York: McGraw-Hill Book Co., 1970.

————. *My Brother Paul.* New York: Harper & Row, 1972.

————. "On Death in Life: Reflections on Franz Rosenzweig." *Soundings,* Vol. 55, No. 2, Summer 1972.

————. *The Cunning of History.* New York: Harper & Row, 1976.

————. *The Religious Imagination.* Indianapolis: The Bobbs-Merrill Company, Inc., 1968.

Sachar, Howard Morley. *The Course of Modern Jewish History.* Cleveland: The World Publishing Company, 1958.

Sanders, Ronald. "Israel at 25." *Midstream,* Vol. XIX, No. 6, June/July 1973.

Schindler, Peter. "Responses of Hasidic Leaders and Hasidism during the Holocaust." Ph.D. dissertation, New York University, 1972.

Schneur Zalman of Liadi. *Likutei Amarim (Tanya).* Trans. by Nissan Mindel. Brooklyn: Kehot Publication Society, 1969.

Scholem, Gershon. *Major Trends in Jewish Mysticism.* New York: Schocken Books, 1946.

————. *On the Kabbalah and Its Symbolism.* New York: Schocken Books, 1965.

————. *Shabatai Zevi: The Mystical Messiah.* Princeton: Princeton University Press, 1973.

————. *The Kabbalah.* New York: Quadrangle Books, 1974.

————. *The Messianic Idea in Judaism.* New York: Schocken Books, 1971.

Schwarz-Bart, Andre. *The Last of the Just.* New York: Bantam Books, 1961.

Schwarzschild, Steven. "Jewish Values in the Post-Holocaust Future." *Judaism,* Vol. 16, No. 3, Summer 1967.

————. "Toward Jewish Unity." *Judaism,* Vol. 15, No. 2, Spring 1966.

Shazar, Zalman. *Morning Stars.* Philadelphia: The Jewish Publication Society, 1967.

Sherwin, Byron L. "Elie Wiesel and Jewish Theology." *Judaism,* Vol. 18, No. 1, Winter 1969.

————. "Elie Wiesel on Madness." *Central Conference of American Rabbis Journal,* Vol. 20, No. 2, June 1972.

Silberman, Lou H. "Concerning Jewish Theology in North America: Some Notes on a Decade." *The American Jewish Yearbook,* Vol. LXX, 1969.

Silverman, Morris. *The Passover Haggadah.* Hartford: Prayer Book Press, 1959.

Simon, Ernst, and Donat, Alexander. "Revisionist History of the Jewish Catastrophe: Two Examinations of Hannah Arendt." *Judaism,* Vol. XII, No. 4, Fall 1973.

Singer, Isaac Bashevis. *Enemies: A Love Story.* New York: Farrar, Straus, and Giroux, 1972.

————. *The Manor.* New York: Farrar, Straus, and Giroux, 1967.

————. *The Seance.* New York: Farrar, Straus, and Giroux, 1964.

Soloveichik, Joseph Baer. "Confrontations." *Tradition,* Vol. 7, No. 3, Summer 1964.

Spiegel, Shalom. *The Last Trial.* New York: Schocken Books, 1969.

Steiner, Jean Francois. *Treblinka.* New York: New American Library, 1968.

The Babylonian Talmud. English translation edited by I. Epstein. London: Soncino Press, 1935–1948.

Torres, Tereska. *The Open Doors.* New York: Simon & Schuster, 1968.

Trunk, Isaiah. *Judenrat.* New York: The Macmillan Co., 1972.

————. "Religious Education and Cultural Problems in the East

European Ghettoes under German Occupation." *YIVO Annual of Jewish Social Sciences,* Vol. XIV, 1969.

Weiss, J. S. "The Question in Rabbi Nachman's Teaching." *Zion,* Vol. 16, 1951.

Werblowsky, R. J. Zvi. "Faith, Hope, and Trust — An Analysis of the Concept of Bittachon." *Annual of Jewish Studies,* Vol. 2, 1964.

Wiesel, Elie. *A Beggar in Jerusalem.* New York: Random House, 1970.

———. *A Jew Today.* New York: Random House, 1978.

———. *Ani Maamin: A Song Lost and Found Again.* New York: Random House, 1973.

———. *Dawn.* New York: Hill and Wang, 1961.

———. *Four Hasidic Masters and Their Struggle Against Melancholy.* Notre Dame: University of Notre Dame Press, 1978.

———. *Legends of Our Time.* New York: Holt, Rinehart and Winston, 1968.

———. *Messengers of God: Biblical Portraits and Legends.* New York: Random House, 1976.

———. *Night.* New York: Hill and Wang, 1960.

———. *One Generation After.* New York: Random House, 1970.

———. *Souls on Fire.* New York: Random House, 1972.

———. *The Accident.* New York: Hill and Wang, 1962.

———. *The Gates of the Forest.* New York: Holt, Rinehart and Winston, 1966.

———. *The Jews of Silence.* New York: Holt, Rinehart and Winston, 1966.

———. *The Oath.* New York: Random House, 1973.

———. *The Town Beyond the Wall.* New York: Holt, Rinehart and Winston, 1964.

———. *Zalmen, or The Madness of God.* New York: Random House, 1975.

Wyschogrod, Michael. "Faith and the Holocaust." *Judaism,* Vol. 20, No. 3, Summer 1970.

Zborowshi, Mark, and Herzog, Elizabeth. *Life Is with People.* New York: Schocken Books, 1952.

Zimmels, H. J. *The Echo of the Nazi Holocaust in Rabbinic Literature.* New York: Ktav Publishing House, 1977.

The Zohar. Trans. by Harry Sperling and Maurice Simon. 5 volumes. London: Soncino Press, 1933–1934.

Index

Abraham, 109, 112, 113, 114, 120, 174; as first believer, 115
Accident, The. See Le Jour
Adam, 120
Additional covenant, 133, 141, 144, 145, 148, 158; elements of,
    127–29
After Auschwitz (Rubenstein), 153
Akedah, as precursor of Holocaust, 119
Akivah, Rabbi, 122
Alienation, 19
Alter, Robert, 74, 79
Ani Maamin, 69, 91, 103, 109–17
Anomie, 12, 17, 68, 188
Anti-Semitism, 138–46, 141, 197–98
Arendt, Hannah, 7, 137, 181–82, 194–200
Auschwitz, 4, 6, 15, 16, 17, 33, 48, 77, 78, 81, 94, 118; lesson of,
    35; mystery as, 58; precedent as, 36; voice of, 155, 157, 159,
    163, 186

Baal Shem Tov, The, 86, 87, 89; founder of Hasidism, 83
Bakan, David, 98, 199
Beggar: place and role of, 71; symbolic significance of, 72–75
Beggar in Jerusalem, A (Weisel), 65, 69–80, 86, 104
Berger, Peter, 9, 164 n. 29
Berkovits, Eliezer, 7, 111, 152–53, 162, 169, 172–80, 201; chosen-

ness and, 174; galut and, 174; God shackled and, 173; Israel
     and, 175; powerlessness and, 176
Bettelheim, Bruno, 7, 181, 182, 183–85; analytic mode of, 184,
     188, 194, 200; critique of Frank family, 183; on Jewish
     repression, 183–84
Borowitz, Eugene, 161
Buber, Martin, 152
Buchenwald, 3

Cain, 120
Camus, Albert, 39, 139
Cargas, Harry, 86
Community, 68
Chaos, 6
Cone, James, 134, 149, 150

Daly, Mary, 134, 149
Dawidowicz, Lucy, 7, 187–88
Dawn (Wiesel) 9, 25, 26, 30, 42, 60, 70, 79, 84, 85, 100, 130–31,
     150; theodicy in, 21–25
Death, 9, 29, 90, 95; enemy as, 101; futility of, 94; God's last word
     as, 40; premature, 39; protest against, 92; relief as, 100
Donat, Alexander, 195

Eckardt, A. Roy, 77
Eclipse of God (Buber), 152
Education, religious, 66–67
Eichmann, Adolph, 195, 198
Eichmann in Jerusalem (Arendt), 194, 196
Elijah, 24
Elisha, 24, 26–27
Elisha ben Abuyah, 24–25, 26
Evil: God's creation as, 16–17; persistence of, 39; religious prob-
     lem of, 12

Fackenheim, Emil, 6, 7, 94, 128, 152–53, 154–60, 162, 172, 179,
     180; critique of, 156; theodicy of Israel and, 154; viability of
     Midrashic tradition and, 156–58
Faith, 10, 11, 54; life of, 18; inadequacy of, 12; rejection of, 20–21

Faith after the Holocaust (Berkovits), 172
Frankl, Viktor, 141
Freud, Sigmund, 98, 99, 137, 163, 167
Friedman, Maurice, 167
Friendship, 37, 38, 40, 68

Gamaliel, 174
Gates of the Forest, The (Wiesel), 52–68, 71, 82, 89, 100, 102, 104, 185; affirmation of love in, 62–64; reconciliation in, 55
God, 6, 11, 22, 44, 46, 79; absence of, 6, 10, 21, 22, 28, 30; burden of, 18; death of, 22–23, 25, 27, 45; as guilty, 53–56; justice of, 18; negative images of, 28, 29, 42, 45, 117, 179; present in history, 153; present in His People, 173; resisted, 87–88
Guilt of survivors, 191

Halpern, Irving, 55
Hanukkah, 129, 158
Harry James Cargas in Conversation with Elie Wiesel (Cargas), 86
Hasidic tales, 42, 80, 81–82
Hasidism, 53, 80–81, 84, 85, 171; cosmos and, 85; individual and, 82, 85; mystery of, 57; Wiesel's interpretation of, 86; and worldview, 132
Hegel, G. W. F., 10, 163, 167, 174
Heresy, 7, 50
Heretic, 52
Herzog, Elizabeth, 71
Heterodoxy, 7
Hilberg, Raul, 7, 137, 182, 197
Hillel, 174
History, 16, 22, 23, 63; lessons of, 83; human responsibility and, 173
Holidays, the, 12
Holocaust, 6, 7, 9, 15, 27, 37, 69, 76, 80, 92, 110, 113, 128, 129, 144, 189–94, 197; as central to Jewish theology, 152–53; as communal event, 42; God's presence in, 155; Israel and, 37; messengers of God in, 119–20; mystery of, 182, 193; proof of Western decadence, 135–37; response of Hasidism to, 56; as source of guilt, 190–91; unprecedented nature of, 118; world responsibility for, 190

Hope, grounds for, 7
Humanity, 57
Human spirit: origin of all events, 87; as theological center, 74

Indinopulos, Thomas, 54, 167
Isaac, 110, 120, 121, 194; as first surivor, 115
Israel, 6, 11, 12, 14, 17, 27, 36, 157, 164, 171, 178; as answer to
    Holocaust, 37; centrality of, 18, 34, 125; covenant and, 125;
    criticism of, 150; Jewishness of, 132, 151; mission of, 34,
    127; opposition to, 138; as sinner, 12–13; State of, 27, 36,
    113, 148–49, 212; solidarity of, 134; as victim, 18; as pivotal
    to world surival, 173–74; nuclear potential and, 176
Israelis, 70

Jacob, 110, 115
Jerusalem, 78, 79
"Jerusalem, the Symbol of Survival" (Wiesel), 72
Jesus, 33, 139–40
Jews of Silence, The (Wiesel), 103, 132
Job, 14, 15, 112, 113, 123; as unreconciled, 50 n. 34, 51; as
    survivor, 119
Jones, William, 134
Joseph, 101, 122
Joyce, James, 167
Judaism, 14, 30
Judenrat (Trunk), 195

Kabbalah, 11, 22, 49
Kabbalism, Lurrianic, 28, 62, 96, 126, 163
Kaddish, 17, 54, 58, 63; as source of continuity, 59
Kalman, 64, 138
Kaplan, Mordecai, 170
Kierkegaard, Sören, 168
Kotzker, Rebbe, 87

Laughter, task of, 79
Legends of Our Time (Wiesel), 53, 58, 59, 63–64, 103, 185
Le Jour (*The Accident*) (Wiesel), 9, 25–30, 32, 37–38, 43, 44,
    60–62, 70, 100

Levi Yitchak of Berdichiv, Rebbe, 89
Life, as question, 41
Lind, Jakov, 81

Madness, 6, 11, 69–70, 92, 102–3, 104–9
Magid of Mezeritch, 83
Maidanek, 59
Marcuse, Herbert, 104
Marx, Karl, 57–58
Master, 38, 55
Meaning, 41, 42, 58
Melville, Herman, 167
Memory: as cause of anti-Semitism, 138; Jewish, 93
Messengers of God (Wiesel), 91, 103, 117–24, 146, 147
Messiah, 14, 15, 24, 49, 58, 84, 89, 148, 112–13, 116; as unacceptable, 114; Jesus and, 140; narrowed vision of, 95
Messianic future, 15, 16
Messianic moments, 96
Messianism, 84–85
Midrash, 42, 110, 117, 123, 156, 157; collapse of framework of, 128–29
"Moscow Revisited" in *Legends of Our Time* (Wiesel), 103
Moses, 110, 121, 122
Moses and Monotheism (Freud), 98
Mystic, 165–66
"My Teachers" (Wiesel), 13

Nachman of Bratzlav, Rabbi, 11 n. 7, 88, 105
Nausea (Sartre), 40
Neusner, Jacob, 161
New Year, the, 18–19
Nietzsche, Friedrich, 168
Night (Wiesel), 9, 10–21, 22, 29, 44, 54, 69, 83, 100, 103, 121, 142, 178, 182, 185, 186, 188, 189
Noah, 119

Oath, The (Wiesel), 40, 69, 91–102, 103, 105, 122, 143, 146, 159
Omnipotence, quest for, 46–47, 48
One Generation After (Wiesel), 36, 93, 97, 142

"On Jewish Values in the Post-Holocaust Future" (Wiesel), 148
"Orphan, The" (Wiesel), 66

Palestine, 21
Pardes, 192
Passover, 158, 186
"Plea for Survivors, A" (Wiesel), 194
"Plea for the Dead, A" (Wiesel), 194
Prophet, 11
Purim, 129, 158

Raba, 14
Rabbinic legend, 73, 74
Rachel, 110
Rebbe, 60; relationship to community, 57; role of, 55
Reconciliation, partial, 60
Reina, Joseph de la, 84
"Religious Authority and Mysticism" (Scholem), 165
Religious Imagination, The (Rubenstein), 170
Rose, Marion Erster (Mrs. Elie Wiesel), 5
Rubenstein, Richard, 7, 13 n. 9, 111, 137, 152, 153, 157, 160–72,
    178, 179, 180, 182, 200; Jewish reaction to, 160–62; response
    to Auschwitz, 161; concurrence between Wiesel and, 164;
    non-Jewishness of, 167–68; rejection of Jewish forms, 168;
    on Israel, 168; and Christianity, 168–69

Sabbateanism, 84
Sanctification: additional covenant in, 146; defined, 147
Sanders, Ronald, 150–51
Sartre, Jean Paul, 40
Schacter, Zalman, 13 n. 9
Scholem, Gershom, 14, 105, 126, 165–66, 167
Schwarzchild, Steven, 5
Security, sources of, 6
Shekinah, 11, 71
Sherwin, Byron, 34, 36, 37, 77, 78
Sighet, 3, 11, 12, 32, 185, 186, 190
Silence, 97–98, 99, 122, 192
Sinai, 77, 78, 79, 141, 147, 156–57

Six Day War, 73, 133, 149, 150, 153; Torah and, 77
Solidarity, 137, 140–41; survival theology and, 134–35; power of, 191
Solzhenitsyn, Alexander, 139
Soul of Wood (Lind), 81
Souls on Fire (Wiesel), 80–90, 103, 104, 118, 146, 148; alternate title, 81
Soviet Jews, 131, 133, 148, 160, 171; cultural renaissance of, 132
Suffering, 31, 32, 33, 37

Tal, Uriel, 137
Tales, 89
Talmud, 11, 151, 172
Theology, Jewish, 42
Tikkun, 126, 148
Torah, 6, 34, 64, 77–78, 88, 122
Town Beyond the Wall, The (Wiesel), 31–51, 52, 69, 95, 100, 104, 146, 185
Tradition, 7, 12, 20, 23, 24, 78, 84, 106; change of meaning, 59; Israel and, 125; reappropriation of, 52; solidarity in, 133; vis-à-vis Jewish condition, 99
Treblinka, 59

Void, 6, 20, 63, 79

Wertmuller, Lina, *Seven Beauties*, 75
Western Wall, 71, 76, 77, 132
Wiesel, Elie, 33, 43, 67, 159, 160, 171, 189, 190, 192; biography of, 3–4, 63–68; as Jewish symbol, 95, 167; language of, 5, 6, 43, 182; literary genre of, 6, 8 n. 6, 103, 178; literary style, 14; theodicy of, 17, 18, 100, 102, 110, 111–17, 134, 177, 180. Works: *Ani Maamin*, 69, 91, 103, 109–17; *Beggar in Jerusalem, A*, 65, 69–80, 86, 104; *Dawn*, 9, 21–25, 26, 30, 42, 60, 70, 79, 84, 85, 100, 130–31, 150; *Gates of the Forest, The*, 52–68, 71, 82, 89, 100, 102, 104, 185; *Legends in Our Time*, 53, 58, 59, 63–64, 103, 185; *Le Jour*, 9, 25–30, 32, 37–38, 43, 44, 60–62, 70; *Messengers of God*, 91, 103, 117–24, 146, 147; *Night*, 9, 10–21, 22, 29, 44, 54, 69, 83, 100, 103, 121, 142, 178, 182, 185, 186, 188, 189; *Oath, The*, 40, 69,

91–102, 103, 105, 122, 143, 146, 159; *One Generation After,*
36, 93, 97, 142; *Souls on Fire,* 80–89, 103, 104, 118, 146, 148;
Town Beyond the Wall, The, 31–51, 52, 69, 95, 100, 104, 146,
185; *Zalmen, or the Madness of God,* 40, 91, 102–9, 146, 147
Wiesel, Shlomo Elisha (son), 5
Witness, 92, 94, 100; difficulty of, 141; extent of, 144, 145; Wiesel
    as, 143
Wizsnitz, Rebbe of, 65
Wyschograd, Michael, 158–59, 160, 177

Yom Kippur, 19–20, 105, 107
Yom Kippur War, 176

Zaddik, 48
Zalman, Rabbi Scheneor, 126, 127
Zalmen, or the Madness of God (Wiesel), 40, 91, 102–9, 146, 147
Zbarainski, Mark, 71
Zohar, The, 16